Sources of Love and Peace

by Sabine Lichtenfels

Translated from the German by
Sten Linnander and Kate Bunney

VERLAG MEIGA

2. Edition
© 2010 Verlag Meiga
Waldsiedlung 15
D-14806 Belzig
Tel: +49 (0) 3 38 41 3 05 38
Fax: +49 (0) 3 38 41 3 85 50
Email: info@verlag-meiga.org
www. verlag-meiga.org

Translated from the German by Sten Linnander and
Kate Bunney

Original title:
Quellen der Liebe und des Friedens. Morgenandachten.
Belzig, 2001.
Printed by Lightning Source Ltd. UK/USA

All drawings by Sabine Lichtenfels
Cover-Design: Juliane Paul

ISBN: 978-3-927266-11-7

Content

Content

Foreword

"For where two or three are gathered together in my name, there am I in the midst of them." These words by Jesus have been with me since my early youth. As a theologian and friend of original Christianity, I have for many years been engaged in peace work. My most important goal is the dissolution of fear and the creation of trust, both between human beings and between humans and their co-creatures. All beings can become partners in the worldwide work for peace, if they can connect with each other in trust. When I am in prayer, I often receive inspirations regarding this topic.

I live in a community in Portugal, in which new paths in the area of the healing of the human being and of nature are being developed and tested. Currently, about 50 people live in this community, which has no religious affiliation, but where all members actively follow their own spiritual paths. Many have had religious experiences that have connected them to the unity of Creation.

Many orient themselves toward the original Christian values of truth, trust, love and non-violence toward all creatures. For a long time now, I have spoken the morning prayers every morning. Whereas in the beginning I had to find the right words to say and prepare a text in advance, suddenly the words began to come by themselves. They came so quickly and so unequivocally that I only had to "take them down" every morning before prayers. What came were messages that I feel are so relevant to our future that I want to pass them on.

If we allow ourselves to fully receive these messages, then a peace-generating power enters into our souls. The messages tell us that the information of peace and healing already now is present and accessible. Every day they tell us anew that we carry the Divine within us and that we have the power to realize it. We have the real possibility to make a decision for peace, here and now. It is a decision for trust and against fear, for solidarity and against hatred.

It is your decision to live in the name of peace. Peace can occur through you, here and now. It wants to be understood and realized here on earth, not in the beyond. Stop your habit of projecting your longings into a distant future. Learn to live at a high level of presence. Live in the expectation of a fulfilling presence.

I am a woman. Maybe that is why the source of the messages often appears to me in the form of a Goddess, as the female aspect of God. All material life seems to me to be pulsating with the energies of a female deity, sometimes appearing spiritually in front of me with very personal features. The old matriarchal peoples of early history probably had similar experiences when praying to Isis, Freya, Ischtar or Nammu. It is a very vital and highly present appearance of the Divine. I might add, as a theologian, that even in the Bible, the Holy Ghost sometimes appears in a female form. In the Christian gnosis and in the tradition of the Russian Orthodox Church, the female aspect of God has remained in the form of Sophia or Sophia-Maria. In the tradition of the Catholic Church, Maria, as "the Mother of God" has a similarly high religious status. But ultimately God is not tied to any gender, name, concept, culture or time. I ask the reader not to be irritated by the female form that I have chosen. We should all choose those images that give us the greatest power and trust. After all, these are our projections, for God is neither male nor female. God/dess is the soul of the world that lives and operates in all things and yet stands above all things. God/dess is the highest authority of Creation and of love, connecting all beings to each other, calling us to make contact with her/him. If we allow this connection with the soul of the world to occur, we will notice that it can speak to us in a very living way. In the morning prayers, it speaks to us repeatedly in the "I" form, which reminded me of the "I am" statements in the Gospel according to John. In this "personal" contact with the soul of the world, we experience messages that we alone would never have thought of, for example about the inner connections between erotic and religious life.

One may be surprised that there are statements about sexuality and love in a prayer book. There is a connection in our souls between Eros and altruism, and an essential contribution to peace and healing on our earth consists of re-balancing the universal male and female forces. They should follow the principle of complementarity instead of that of domination. One reason for human violence is that these forces have lost their natural balance and are fighting each other instead of inspiring and loving each other. The idea of dominance and subordination lies deep in our cells and has left deep wounds. Instead, we should carefully raise our heads into the light of a Creation that lies outside of such categories, for we constantly carry the building plan of love within us. If we enter this inner plan, it is as if we pass through a gate into a new reality. We are challenged to step out both from the spirit of fear and the spirit of anger and revenge and recognize an entirely different reality. We then leave all resentment and power games between man and woman behind us, for we see the beauty and the deep peace that lies in the fact that they complement each other.

I once stood at the threshold of death, and since then I feel repeatedly challenged to open up spiritual doors and overcome, already in this earthly life, the blocks that separate us from truth. I have been privileged to look into the gifts of love that have been given to man and woman. Religions have done much to suppress these gifts. May a new spirit now contribute to bringing them to light again. We need truth and divine guidance, also specifically in the area of sensuality, for here the greatest joy and the greatest pain lie close together. I am especially grateful for the inspiration that these morning prayers provide in this area.

Imagine that you come to a gate. You open it and enter into the beyond. The beyond is paradise and this paradise is – the earth. Could not the earth turn into a paradise if we learn to understand and accept the laws of happiness? Could not much healing occur if we again understand that the living spirit of Eros cannot be tied to two people, but was created for the universal celebration of Creation?

This book is intended as a book of meditation. The intent of its 52 morning prayers – one new message of peace and one power sentence for every week of the year – is to let us see and understand our everyday issues on a deeper and more encompassing level. The texts can liberate us from our habitual fixation on problems and create a new opening for solutions to emerge. Since the texts arose during a number of community meetings, they partially mirror the concrete spirit of community life. But they primarily mirror the universal Spirit of Creation, which can help and heal in all situations in life.

I propose the creation of a conscious, worldwide project, in which we reconnect with the elementary powers of Creation and understand that the earth with all its creatures is a breathing, communicating, divine, living being that is based on trust and cooperation. Every being that swims, crawls, walks or flies on earth is an aspect of the one divine life and wants to participate in the joy of existence.

Everything wants to live in the great connection that
we call love. May these morning prayers contribute
to making this happen.

Thank you and Amen.
Ya azim: I greet the Divine in you.

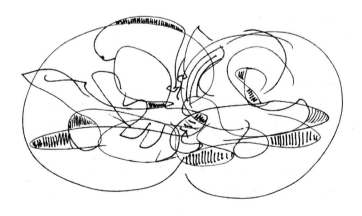

Cooperation with Cosmic Forces

Understanding Prayer

There are spiritual energies that can be accessed everywhere in the world – forces of consciousness are at work everywhere. The human being can perceive these forces of consciousness and enter into cooperation with them. Prayer research means that I enter into resonance with the vibrational pattern of universal information. I step out of the kind of thinking that comes from separation and definitions and begin to perceive and cooperate with all forces of consciousness.

In prayer we can study and learn to understand the logic of universal love.

In prayer we connect with the thinking power of the heart.

There is neither a God outside of the human being, nor is there no God. The universal divine aspect of Creation wants to realized through us humans. This is a dialectic process of becoming. The Divine is the highest creative and spiritual goal image of the entire universe and of all things becoming. The human being has the task of bringing this power of consciousness onto earth and realizing it.

As a collective, we have gone through a phase of atheism, which was triggered by Marx, Nietzsche and others. Religion was seen as opium for the people. This historic phase was perhaps necessary in order to thoroughly clean out the history of religion from which we come. Countless wars have been fought due to a false image of religion. This God of Terror came about through the focused power of humans, who gave birth to him and strengthened him as an idea. They managed to get millions of people to pray to him, thus bringing forth his cruel effects. What was called forth was not the spirit of love; it was the spirit of punishment, power and suppression. Cultures always gained power by creating highly effective icons.

Healing does not occur so much by abolishing religion. Life itself has a religious aspect. We are faced with the challenge of honoring the sacred quality of life and giving it back the position it deserves. We can again step into the miracle of Creation and perception. We can consciously access the universal powers of consciousness that we desire and that serve the humanity of life. Here, too, the dialectic principle applies. It is up to us to decide which universal powers we invoke and realize. We must therefore, of course, free ourselves from all old religious and moral ideas and from ideas that are hostile to love, as well as from the punishing God that is still latently operating in us. We must discover what the universal power of love might be and how it can operate. A humane God or an all-embracing, loving Mother Goddess already exists in the highest longing of human beings. The divine power of a humane world is becoming more and more concrete, and it is giving birth to a new force of peace from a new and higher principle. Here, the power of the world and that of humans will unite in their purest form and highest potency.

The world of universal consciousness does not want us to be small and subjugated, but in our full divine presence and power of realization. In this sense, the human being needs the humane divine power and God needs humans for his/her own realization. Those who desire a humane world and still believe in its fulfillment will explore the inner spaces of resonance, through which this cooperation can come about. For it is only through this process that field-generating and healing changes can come about.

The idea that there is a humane consciousness in the universe is the strongest driving force for its realization. Our full connection with this idea brings forth the strongest power, the highest will, and the greatest trust. By taking a stand for our own full connection with this idea, it becomes a very personal experience of God, an endless source of power. Ultimately, trust is only possible in connection with this divine humane source. It is the source of our creative actions. This is where the dialectic principle of Creator and Creation is realized. The idea of a religion of Creation is a better description of this process than that of a religion of salvation, which promises us a paradise beyond and a God outside of ourselves in order to make us submissive and governable here on earth.

In prayer, an essential source of power is to give thanks. It is often only by giving thanks that I begin to perceive fully what the world is presenting to me. One early morning I got the message "Give – take – give thanks". This is the most elementary way of describing the process of every prayer.

In addition to giving, asking is an important element in prayer. Inform the Cosmos of what you truly want and need, and you will receive it. The Cosmos does not react to servility and begging; it needs free human beings who inform it clearly and simply. It is up to us to formulate our wishes so unequivocally that they can be understood. If secret desires and fears oppose the request we formulate, then this causes "static on the line". The world cannot answer then, for the channels of information are blocked.

A further essential element in prayer is the lack of inner contradictions. If, for example, I am full of violence without knowing it, then I cannot pray effectively for peace. Intensive prayer research automatically leads to self-transformation. We encounter many beliefs, dogmas and old fears that prevent us from realizing our own true, higher gestalt. Prayer research is therefore always also consciousness research concerning the processes of one's own soul. There will be no peace on earth as long as there is war within us. Those who are against war, need a vision for peace, also for their own peace.

It is therefore important for all peace work that we begin to develop images of an encompassing peace. We are challenged to take these images and our true longings that are resonating latently in our souls seriously and transform them into effective icons. In its most encompassing form, prayer unites with the visionary power of a new Creation. This new Creation is not arbitrary; instead, it emerges from the already existing powers of Creation and from cooperation with it.

These morning prayers are, of course, not tied to any specific concepts of God or to any specific belief system. Nobody has to believe in God in order to pray. But one must have the absolute will to open up new fields of consciousness, question old beliefs, and rid oneself of prejudice. An atheist can use these morning prayers as a source of power just as well as a believer. My language may color the prayers a certain way – but everyone will know what is meant.

During morning prayers I consciously experience that I am embedded in a larger whole, the Universe. I experience myself as being an essential participant in the process of Creation, and I experience the connectedness of all things. This perception draws me into a great universal energy circulation.

During meditation I experience that the entire biosphere is designed on the basis of trust and communication. When I am in a state of trust, I communicate differently than in a state of mistrust or fear. When I am trusting, I open all my senses toward the world; if, however, I fear or distrust, my organs of communication immediately close off and I am no longer open to perceive. Each type of communication that I choose brings about a different reality. Practicing trust is an essential aspect of prayer research. It is a matter of decision whether to walk the path of trust or not.

The human being's universal powers of consciousness are dependent on feedback and information. The source of this consciousness must be used, or else it will become stale. The human being is an essential part of this source and its constant transformation and renewal. If the human being does not inform and provide feedback, then this part is missing in the chain of information, resulting in faulty developments. Figuratively speaking one can say that the computer has not received the necessary input and therefore produces false results. The resulting illnesses are seen as healthy and normal.

The human being has forgotten his/her spiritual origin and the spiritual world has forgotten the material state of being. The forgetting is equally great on both sides. Prayer is work to reestablish a natural connection. Continuity in prayer allows us to remember and become conscious of our own origins, our will and our true goal.

In this sense, life itself ultimately becomes our prayer, in that we constantly train our powers of trust. Life itself has an answer for us, if we want to hear it. I have often experienced this connection in situations of distress. As long as I cling to my distress, the universal reality of love cannot reach me. Divine life is therefore always a process of communication between the human being and the world. True prayer means to enter into the process of Creation as a fully participating and responsible person. This is our task, our duty and, at the same time, our freedom. This is where the historic birth of the humane human being occurs.

I then do not have to sit down, close my eyes and pray. In a state of connectedness, every bird's song, every telephone call and every encounter holds meaning and promise.

It is only when our senses have become free that we can see the state of fear in which the beings on the entire earth find themselves. If we begin to take spiritual research seriously, we automatically become political human beings. We then recognize our task as custodians of the earth, and how essential it is that we become the perceiving and speaking organ that we are meant to be. The emergence of worldwide peace depends on our actions. There is no humane God without human beings. A prayer that comes from love automatically seeks answers to the suppression of life and it seeks to overcome every situation of violence.

An important source for a spiritual way of life lies in the area of Eros. In early cultures, it was natural to hold erotic celebrations as a way of thanking the Goddess and Creation. It was clear that Eros was a divine power and source, and not a personal one. In an erotic life practice, the goal is to bring spiritual knowledge into our bodies and senses. Whether we have success in our erotic life practice essentially determines if we seek our fulfillment in the beyond or in life on earth, if we become clinical and frustrated pragmatists or if we understand to celebrate the miracle of Creation. It is not a question of overcoming sexuality, as many spiritual teachers claim, but one of giving birth to the erotic human being. Eros begins to blossom fully when the human being enters into cosmic consciousness. When that occurs, cosmic love is no longer separated from sensual love.

May the Goddess operate within us and through us. May the forces of a worldwide peace-creating spirit be realized. In the name of a new sensual and spiritual culture, I now give the word in this book to the voice of the Goddess, as I received it during a meditation.

Wars are a result of ideology

Wars were caused by the fear of woman and sensuality. Wars were caused by the fight against the Goddess. The history of the heretics is a history of the suppression of the Goddess. When the first human beings fully remember this knowledge, they will have the power to take Jesus down from the cross. The history of the last 5000 years is stored in your cells as fear. Fear is also a signpost for you. It is the conglomerated, separated part of a long history and a great knowledge that is crying out for redemption in you.

Do not follow fear. This represents a theology of decision that keeps wanting to be understood.

Do not follow the attraction of emotions that have not been recognized and understood, and that for thousands of years has led the human being into the same abyss. The fear in you says: do it differently this time. Become aware of ME. Make sure that you now choose your new steps mindfully. Be neither a hero nor a coward. You need to understand what energies have governed your life subconsciously and separated you from the Goddess.

Truths have been advocated in a harsh way. Truths were carried on banners without being known within. Luther, Müntzer, Calvin, Zwingli: they all joined the same religion. They then entered into an ideological fight, one of rage and hatred. They no longer heard the voice of the Goddess or the song of the birds, which would immediately have made them put down their swords.

Do you think that they would have acted that way if they had known how to truly love their women?

If women were again to learn to truly love their sons, do you think they would allow them to go to war over religion?

Truths were forced into laws and standards, with devastating results. That takes away their freshness of perception and their breath of love. They are thus no longer truths.

The Cathars, who surely had a noble spirit, followed an ideology. They did not know the space of sensuality and gentle power. They did not know the aspect of the Goddess that breathes through everything on earth and that makes truths intimate, flexible and malleable.

They put their love of light above life. They called the God who lives in the beyond and they fulfilled their destiny in a bitter way.

All these historic events require each of you to pause for a long while. And each of you needs to be healed as a result of these events.

Do not follow fear. The protection that you then receive is immeasurable.

Do not follow heroism or the voice of martyrdom in you. The danger that lies here is painful.

The Anabaptists had begun to rediscover the path of sensual love. But they, too, made an ideology of it. The voice of the Goddess, who had just begun to reveal herself to the finer sensual perception, was vehemently attacked. Instead of following a path whereby men once again shyly begin to follow their love, they silenced the female voice in themselves and others and preferred to initiate their own demise with raised banners.

They fought with false means against a world that they had not understood within themselves.

In their ecstatic madness, they had begun to fight each other.

Follow the path that makes it possible for you to understand the balance between your inner processes and the processes in the world and to set a new course here.
Notice that truth shines differently, depending on whose eyes perceives it.
There is only one law of life, and that is the law of love.

Understand the task of the human being as one of caring for the balance between heaven and earth and assuming responsibility. It is fear that makes human beings controllable. It is fear that makes it possible for humans to succumb to the spell of hatred. It is fear that drives heroism.

Do not follow fear any more and you will not follow violence either.

This statement can only be understood on a very deep level. For if you take a stand for violence, then that, too, seems to protect you from fear. However, deep within you, there is a fear virus that you are not aware of and that governs your life until you become seeing and knowing.

If you follow the predator impulse, you will automatically follow the victim impulse too, until you become seeing and knowing.

Make it impossible for people to fight against you with such cruel methods, **by seeing through their methods within yourself and thus abandoning them fully.**

Learn to move about in society without any ideology.

Stop nourishing hostility by not fanning this fire within yourself.

If you follow truth in its movable, flexible, dancing, female and male, perceiving and creative, physical and loving aspects, then you will experience great protection.

You will then find the right words and deeds.

You will then no longer want to change the world by convincing and converting others. You change them by changing yourself, through the power of life itself and through the participation that grows from this.

Of course you are then able to say what you really think without fear. Great heretic figures from the past followed this path into death. They stood under great protection. They did not follow fear, not even in the hour of death. They now carry great knowledge within.

Through their path, the knowledge that for thousands of years has been controlled and banished through fear can now be accessed.

If you redeem this knowledge that was banished in fear, you become a keeper of peace. For here lies great knowledge that for so long has been suppressed by outside hypnosis.

Let this knowledge of peace breathe again by giving life to the Goddess.

I Want to Find an Anchor for a New Creation in You

Open your hearts and bodies, so that the spirit of beauty can enter you.

Let MY words, MY thoughts and MY actions be yours, in your individual and irreplaceable way.

Rise up to the heights of your spirit that lend wings to your soul. Connect with the spiritual place within you, in which the soul of the universe vibrates.

For I am in everything that exists.

Shatter the ego's little cage, in which you see what is small as being large, where your thoughts are heavy and everyday life is grey, because you believe that you are something that you are not, and because you hold on to things that have no permanence.

You are much more than your ego. Let go of false vanity, so that I, the Soul of the World, can operate through you.
I am now.

30

All you need is courage and presence. Everyday anew, learn what it means to connect with ME and to not be fearful of the magnitude of the divine presence that wants to operate through you.

To thine own self be true, and it must follow, as the night the day, thou canst not then be false to any man.

Greet the Divine in everything that you encounter today, and know that I can be found everywhere. **An aspect of MY being shines toward you through everything. When you connect with ME, you will see and understand everything differently, for I am in everything.**

If you are connected with ME, separation or loneliness is an illusion.

Anchor the words, deeds and thoughts that come to you from ME, deep in your heart.

For I am the Soul of the World that wants to operate through you.

I lie behind the landscape of doubt that you have to cross, again and again, in order to fully recognize me. You recognize ME in the elementary power and freedom that comes from ME to you.

I Want to Find an Anchor for a New Creation in You.

The Soul of the World shines through you in your irreplaceable way. You are needed in your true power and beauty, which lies beyond all comparisons.

Wherever you are whole, because I shine through you in full freedom, there you are beautiful, there you are true. There your fear subsides, for you are secure and you are carried within ME. There, your words, thoughts and deeds have an authentic power, because they know how to dance in the divine light. Arise, shine, for thine light cometh.

Here, the miracles that the earth has waited for, for so long, can manifest. **Rise up to the heights of your Spirit where I, the Soul of the World, can operate fully through you.**

Make this divine day your day. It only exists once. Connect already now with the spirit of thankfulness for this day, for thankfulness is a high power of manifestation.

Thank you, ya azim, and Amen!

You are needed in your true power and beauty, which lies beyond all comparisons.

I Am Always Here

I am always here.
There is nothing that is without ME.

It is the chatter of the many dialogues, the jungle of the many projections, and the illusion of separation that keeps you away from ME.

I am constant change. What still separates you from ME is the mind that is unwilling to connect with the constant power of change. If you hold on to the old, the days become arduous and difficult.

You often think that things are very urgent. You begin to rush from one thing to another. And time is truly short. This is why it is so important to find the right speed that comes from your inner calm, so that you are deeply grounded in the power of trust.

Anchor your heart in MY calmness and in MY power.

Connect with the spirit of presence, from which all things happen at the right time.

You can then let go of many things that burden your heart needlessly, and you will act with the highest precision and power.

In ME, things become neither fast nor slow. But they find the necessary lightness, so that they become free to move. They are all born of calm and of power. Trust arises through the right speed.

You will learn this when you connect with the Spirit of the Earth, for it is only here that space and time reign. They are the clothes of the Earth.
Its heartbeat is also your heartbeat; its rhythm is also your rhythm. Its longing is also your longing, and its pain is also your pain, if you are connected with ME.

Make your body a temple of the Divine, and nourish it in this attitude in all ways. Make yourself into a messenger of the divine power, and make your voice its voice.

Swing yourself up to the state where you can understand everything that exists, because you are a part of it. For there is only one existence.

Anchor the divine Eros in yourself, and give it free rein within you. Make its gait your gait; it is present everywhere.

Combined with erotic love, your words and your deeds dance in the divine light of sensual beauty.

The power of trust is infinitely beautiful. Arise, shine; for thy light cometh. Swing yourself up to the realm of your mind where I, the Soul of the World, can operate fully through you.

Thank you, ya azim and Amen!

Anchor your heart in MY calmness and in MY power.

There are no Enemies

Healing only occurs if you accept love.
You will only be able to bring about peace once you
have found peace in yourself.

Peace is inherent within you and within all beings.
Like a seed, it is waiting for you to discover and
develop it. Do whatever you do, with this seed in
you.

It is MY task to be everywhere and in everything. It
is your task to be where you are fully and thereby to
keep your connection to ME. Stay with ME, for I am
everywhere.

I am also where things seem to be facing you in
hostility. Only when you understand that, can the
peace-creating power of the mind manifest in you.

There are no enemies, only potential friends.

Hostility comes from the illusion of separation. If you
have a hostile attitude, then you are separated from
yourself and separated from the one existence. You

have not yet been able to truly see and understand you own negative aspects. You therefore judge them in yourself and others.

Look into the mirror of your own soul. Gather all your courage in order not to get a fright when you see the images that you do not like. Look at them fully. At the deepest point, you will always find your way to ME. Here, you will also find information on how to overcome fear, shock and violence.

Know that you have all been both victim and perpetrator. What you judge in others today you may have been yourself in the past.

The request that you think differently about your enemies only seems moralistic as long as you seek an external God, who stands in judgment over you.

For inside of you, you also have a judge, who stands in judgment over you and others.

That is the God of the Old Testament.
It is your own judging eyes that come from separation.

When you are connected with ME, you can free others from judgment by freeing yourself from it.
If this peace can manifest fully in the souls, the power of change is enormous, for the power of peace is a divine power.

Healing only occurs
if you accept love.

The Caterpillar Carries
the Butterfly within it

A strong power is waiting to be received by you. This power transforms everything, and you see everything in a new light.

It needs your will and your open heart as its birth canal in order to manifest within you. For those who have this will, the whole universe is the placenta for their work.

Realize that a whole universe is dancing in your cells.

But do not think that it is a question of breaking down all limits and boundaries. There is enough time and space for limitless existence in eternity, where there is no time.

But now you are on Earth. Here, the art of appropriate limits is waiting for you.

A form exists due to its limits. A form exists in order to seduce and catch a power. Give your thoughts, your actions and your existence a creative form, by making consciously chosen decisions.

Earthly existence is waiting for the art of seduction to be learned, so as to let the Divine dance in all forms of existence.

Do not look for the Divine behind everything, but discover the Divine that operates within everything. **Do not wait for miracles to happen, but perceive the divine miracle evolving in front of your eyes, every day anew.**

Carry your body like a divine gown that was given to you so that you can experience, see, hear, smell, taste, love and understand life, specifically in this space of existence.

Recognize the possibility for existence and the bliss that lies in this form of existence. Paradise on Earth is still waiting for its fulfilment. This is our common dream, which weaves us together in a collective work of creation.

The feast of earthly love is still waiting for its redemption and fulfilment.
Follow your longing in such a way that you connect with its fulfilment.

This is the path of a new Creation that I walk with you. Every hunger can be fed, every thirst can be quenched, and every longing carries the entelechy of its fulfilment.

The caterpillar carries the information of the butterfly.

It would feel miserable if it constantly longed to be a butterfly and thereby had the feeling that it was banished into the form of a caterpillar. Yet it does not know of this aberration of the mind. Instead, it **is**. A seed carries the complete information of the plant within; it unfolds according to its inner laws of growth.

The same is true for human beings. But the human being has the additional task of understanding and creating anew. The freedom of the mind made it possible for the human being to follow many winding paths and even to destroy him/herself.

Your path will be fulfilled easier and it will be less arduous and more like a dance, if you trust your own fulfilment. If you do not, you are like a plant that disconnects itself from the water it needs for its growth.

It is a decision to take the path of trust.

Ya azim.

> *Follow your longing in such a way*
> *that you connect with its fulfillment.*

Eros and the Vibration
of the Soul of the World

Experience the moment of birth of this new day inside of you. Anchor yourself, again and again, in this silence, when the events of the day begin to let you forget.

Universal love carries the highest power of survival; here, you are safe in the universe. Universal love is the source that can feed you everywhere. When you vibrate in this love, it changes your body, thoughts and actions.

You live in the vibrational frequency of the Soul of the World.
Do you sense the free, wild, and all-embracing dance that your soul is beginning to dance in ME?

I am love, and love is what will survive all doubt, fears, worries and destructive thoughts in you.

It is the source that flows out from ME, when you have found your deepest foundation in ME. Eros is an expression of the dance of MY soul on Earth.

Eros is not something that you can get or possess. But it is with you, when you give its freedom space in your soul.

Eros is an expression of universal love. If you attempt to lock it up, it becomes violent and leads to illness, rage and negation.
If you try to live it without anchoring it in your heart, it becomes destructive, drags your soul away and leads to addiction.

If you follow the voice of Eros from your innermost center, if you open up to its power, knowledge, unpredictability and eternal youth, it leads you from one divine revelation to the next.
If you try to hold on to Eros, you destroy the flight of life itself. But if you kiss joy in midair, you live in the dawn of eternity.

Eros opens the awareness of your body. It is the body's source of love and insight. It connects immediately with the Goddess.

Connected with her, you know when to act and when not to act. Be still and listen to her voice.

For this world was created for Eros. It is Eros.
No soul on earth can be without Eros. Everything was created and born of Eros.

Sexuality is the highest material creative source. There is no human being who did not come from this source.

When you are connected to Eros, you can experience the sensual faithfulness and power of creation of Shakti and Shiva.

In Eros you recognize the free soul of the sacred whore again. She is a source of healing.

Connected with Eros, a man regains his original gentle power and might.

Eros makes the female cells jubilate and dance, and connects them with their deepest knowledge.

In Eros you experience the divine dance of universal love, the divine wedding, which is not tied to conditions, partnership, relationship, beauty or youth.

Eros is the fountain of youth for every cognitive and loving spirit.

Eros is only tied to your opened and loving heart, for its healing power to operate within you.

Ya azim. Stay with ME.
Then I am with you, wherever you may go.

> *Eros is the fountain of youth*
> *for every cognitive and loving spirit.*

Pain of the World

When you open your soul to the divine light in all of existence, you will experience not only that a great joy and power come to you, but also an infinite pain and sadness. You will be touched by divine compassion. **Those who become seeing will not be able to avoid commiserating with all creatures.**

This commiseration is so strong that it threatens to pull you into personal emotions. Outraged that the world is the way it is, you will want to close your heart again. In this distorted mirror of emotions, even the Divine appears cruel and violent to you. But it is the closed off human being who is cruel.

The Soul of the World calls out in you: remain seeing, here too. Remain with ME, here too. Then a new healing power can operate inside of you. Do not destroy what seems to destroy you. Otherwise you will be destroyed. Do not hate what seems to hate you. Otherwise you are on the side of those who hate. Do not close off your heart in fear of the reality that you live in. Hear MY healing call, which calls out for new paths of love, in these processes, too. Love is the only true source of survival. If you remain firm in your heart, then the power of infinite love reigns in your compassion and gives you a new authority to act.

It is especially here that the Soul of the World is waiting for the first humans who do not close themselves off from MY call, so that the work of change can occur. Suffering decreases with every awakened heart. Every dissolution of a boundary opens up a new, greater and more encompassing world in ME.

With ME you can go to the limits of death without fear. You will know yourself when I call you and when it is time to change worlds.
Connected with ME, you receive the protection that you are seeking. In this connection, you can enter the danger zones and bring about something new. Do not follow fear.

MY compassion gives rise to the sacred rage that does not act out of revenge, but that acts with absoluteness.

Every pain that the world has been subjected to is MY pain and therefore also yours.

Once you have seen the misery of the world with MY eyes, you will no longer wait.

You will set off until you have found the answers that connect you with the authority to act.
You will act wherever you can.
You will act with an open heart, and you will see that it is only through trust and in trust that you can be effective.

You will not be able to heal a closed heart, but wherever hearts begin to open again, MY healing power can take effect.
This principle operates until death. There are those who do not become seeing until in the hour of their death. Others resist the law of infinite love even here. Yet there can only be redemption through infinite love.

You become active when you are connected with infinite love. You will then no longer dwell in the feeling of impotence.

The sacred rage that comes from love gives you a power that emphatically rejects everything that does not serve love. You will protect life wherever you are. And you will accompany dying souls and show them the way to where eternal life can be found.

In everything that you meet, you will seek ME. For there is only one existence.

Sacred rage is higher than all violence. It does not judge, it does not reproach, it does not stand in judgment, it does not hate, and it does not follow the energies of revenge. Connected to sacred rage, you will no longer project onto the power of those who follow destruction.

There is a point where they lose their power over you. Here, the power of change prevails. You are protected by being connected to the laws of eternal life.

If you follow this principle of life, you can achieve infinitely much. You even change souls that only know hatred. If, even in the areas of fear and threat, the full and conscious principle of trust can take hold in you, then your power of change is infinite. It operates across generations.

It is the only power that can save and heal this planet.

Love is the only true source of survival.
It is the only power that can save this planet.

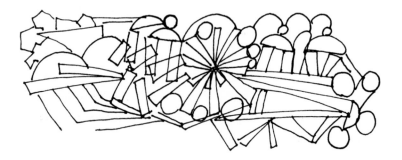

Spiritual Instruction for Peace Workers

Whatever you do, do it fully. Do it from the fullness of your heart.

See to it that you feel good and that it is deeply grounded. In this way you best serve yourself and the world.
Do not be afraid of the difficulties. For every difficulty there is enough power for its solution. Open your heart and be prepared to know; God within you will take care of the rest.

Let go of vanity. Vanity is the attempt by a free soul to fly into an imaginary cage of the ego. As long as your actions depend on the eyes of others, your soul is caught in the cage that you have built yourself. Break open your cage and learn to enter the freedom of dancing, communicating souls.

Acting instead of doing nothing is not vanity. The mistake lies in the faint-heartedness that does not dare do anything. You have already dared to do great things in full freedom, when faint-heartedness had left you.

You are needed at the level where your own inner peace can radiate out into the world to where there is no peace. So find your own voice and make it powerful and clear.

Find the right thoughts that give you power. The right thoughts always lead to actions. Every thought wants to be tested, learned and given birth to.
Take care of the inner structure of your thoughts, for you should know that reality is created from it. A correct thought has an infinitely transforming power.

Accept the mirror that the world is offering you. Here is your reality and here lies your possibility for change and for realizing yourself. Here lies your possibility and your source for bringing the divine love within you into the world.
If you cannot love the world around you, how can you then change the whole? If you cannot love yourself, how can you ever be able to love the world around you?

The world will always mirror back to you what you are yourself. It will mirror infinite peace back to you when you have found peace within yourself. This peace may appear very different from what you think today.

The possibility of peace begins when you stop judging and when you can begin to see, to know and to change, because you have found the power of trust within yourself.

You will find this power when you have looked so deeply into the mirror of your soul that you have found ME again.
If the noble one sees good, he first imitates it; if he has faults, he discards them. Do not cling to your faults, for that is only a waste of time. Here's to our cooperation, ya azim!

Do not cling to your faults,
for that is only a waste of time.

Love and Connectedness

Ya azim.
Wash your face in happiness and health, by taking pleasure in joy.

Always remember that difficulties are overcome with ease. Whenever things have become too difficult to change, humor is the divine source of transformation.

You've got work to do. May this work be your service to the world. May your work be your service of love. May your work serve to lighten up your life. Whatever is done out of love, will have an impact.

Your thoughts, words and deeds have an impact when you are connected with yourself and with the whole.

You are much freer than you think. Go to where your soul has wings.

Whenever your thoughts are critical or even destructive, focus. Connect with the power of transformation where even critical thoughts become a contribution to the creative continuum.

When you need help, call ME. Wait. Know that the Soul of the World is always within you and that it has an answer for you if you allow it to come through.

You can change your whole attitude and point of view in a single moment. Learn to live so that you can.
It is your task to clean up the past, care for the present, and attend to the future. Some people break down when faced with the vastness of this task, whereas others begin to rejoice because of the vastness of these possibilities.

When you let ME in, you begin to become light.

Whatever you now create in terms of peace and what you now can reconcile carries the seed power of a whole world within it and the power of growth for a new becoming.
It is the hour of birth of a new morning and the healing power for your past.

When you find the right thoughts in the stillness of your heart, you can move the whole world as if it is turning in your hand.

Remain connected to serving love.

It protects you from the feeling of separation, from delusions of grandeur and vanity, and also from a false sense of smallness.

Everything that is done out of love, attracts love. Do not let yourself be discouraged if love is not returned immediately. Know that love returns if you stay with love.

The first question is not: Am I loved? The first question is: How do I learn to understand the laws of love that want to operate through me? The laws of love transcend all separation. The powers of love can soothe all pain. The powers of love can wipe out guilt.

If you are connected with love, there can be true forgiveness, for suddenly you see through the eyes of the other.

By giving another the attention and the way of seeing that comes from love, his eyes, too, open to new insights.

Ya azim. Blessed be this day.

You are much freer than you think.
Go to where your soul has wings.

How to Relate to Supposed Enemies

There are no enemies, there are only potential friends.

You can be certain that former friends are among those who are fighting you today. You can be certain that former enemies are among those who love you today. You can be certain that you have once fought what is fighting you today.

It is also possible that you yourself have once been someone whom you would see as an enemy today.

You can be certain that your enemies, too, serve your own development, if you remain connected with the Soul of the World.

In the long term, there is only the path of reconciliation, for there is only one existence.

Recognize the enemy within you. Recognize the enemy in your best friends and learn to conquer him – then you will recognize your potential friend in your enemies.

Do not give their hating eyes any nourishment through your fear. Know that also from their hatred a longing calls out for love to be lived.

Fear results in constriction and constriction leads to violence.

It is important that you first of all become still. If you have not truly become still within, every reaction nourishes hostility.

Do not nourish their fire of hatred, which comes from destructive passion, through your premature anger.

You know well enough the hopelessness of an anger that turns you into a puppet of your emotions. Then you have long ago given your power away.
Sacred rage does not hate. It is not attached to the chain of reactions. It comes to you when you have become still enough.

Do not meet your supposed enemy at a common level, for that is the level of opposition: good against evil, growth against destruction, peace against violence.

Go to the level where all opposites are neutralized. Meet your supposed enemy from this place, with the humor, effortlessness and power that carry the power of transformation.

Take their challenge as your own challenge, or as "tyrants", as Castaneda describes it. Take away the projection surface from your opponent by taking back everything that you are projecting onto him.

Take a long, calm look at the drama of how he sees you through his eyes, without being alarmed.
Watch it in closer and closer detail; then you will discover at what point you can disarm him.

You then also know what he loves in you, what he is seeking in you, and what he is provoking in you. **Recognize how you yourself have provoked the opposites in your thoughts and words.**

Opposites are necessary to keep the game of life vital. But there is something behind all opposites that unites them, something that gives them a tension and a distance, through which their polarity serves the cause of peace.

If you want to realize peace, you must get to know the levels where you yourself are not identified with the opposites.

Act from the place where they dissolve into a new synthesis.

Find the place where you no longer relate to your opponent. Use his challenge to come to terms with yourself, by now knowing what you truly are and love.

Once you have dealt with him within yourself, once you have used his attacks for your own growth like an aikido fighter, then act. Now act fully, the way you feel is right.

Retake the power fully. Do not allow any fear into your words and deeds.

You will notice how you have grown through this process. You may have become quieter and gentler. But also more knowing and more encompassing. MY protective spirit will now be able to encompass and change more "world" within you.

You have befriended many an enemy in this way. Do not follow the path of the hero.
Do not follow the path of the martyr.

But walk your path with a steady direction, the path of love, of sacred rage and of overcoming fear.

This path leads with certainty to the goal. It carries the power of transformation and of shining for many people.

Walk the path of the blind master, who follows the light of insight, even in the greatest darkness.

When you arrive at the bottom of your heart, where your heart is still, you will disarm your opponents, because you no longer provide them with a surface for attack.

You will recognize the projection of your own soul in every opponent, and you will know his/her true seeking and longing.

The best resource to realize this is your own humor and your undeviating joy of life.

In the name of healing and the power of transformation. Ya azim.

Retake the power fully. Do not allow any fear into your words and deeds.

I Am Your Highest Duty

May your day be MY day; may MY day be your day.

May every one of your days be a new discovery and our joint feast.

Do not accept the excuse any more that it is not possible due to your many duties.

I am your highest duty; you find ME within every true duty.

Connect with MY becoming and the entire wisdom of Creation is at your disposal. You only live this life once; it would be absurd to miss out on it.

As long as you fight against ME, you are fighting a losing battle. **Together with ME, you shine with the wisdom of your own heart.**

Why do you make problems for yourself, where there are none? The world is full enough of sorrow and pain, most of which has been caused by ignorance about the process of Creation.

Creation needs your free, open, and courageous heart, so that you can create a new Earth and a new Heaven together with ME.

I can do nothing without human beings, for the freedom to be for or against Creation lies within human beings themselves. But the human being cannot, in the long run also, achieve anything without ME.

I am not a God behind all things. Every seeing human being finds ME in all of existence.

I tell you again: Love is not something that one has to receive, that one has to fight for, that one has to divide into parts, like a cake, and that one has to hold on to and defend like a fortress. Love is endless.
Love is I.

If you try to cling to the old when change occurs, you will lose ME and become miserable.

When you change with ME, you remain connected with the spiritual laws of the joy of life and power.

There is always enough, when you are connected with ME. How to recognize ME, always and everywhere, is a matter of learning.

Do not let yourself be tied down in the anxious cage of a relationship. Overcome your pride and make yourself free for the laws of universal love.

Learn the laws of true faithfulness by beginning to truly love one human being.

You will only be able to do this by beginning to truly love ME. For as soon as you become aware of the aspects that you do not love in the other, you want to turn away.

As long as you run away from the aspects that you feel are ugly, you will not find fulfillment. Be still and connect with ME. I carry within ME the laws of a deep faithfulness.

The world is seeking true partnership and free love. Let MY light shine through you. In this way you will be led to those encounters that are destined for you, and to your friends who for a long time have been waiting to be your real friends.

The faithfulness, the certitude, the opening of your heart, trust, and fulfillment cannot be found outside of you; you will find them in ME. That is within you. When you have found it there, you will find it in the world. Connect with this inner willingness to be the happy being that you are. That is your source of power for all your tasks in the world.

If it seems difficult to you, then let art assist you. **You can create love**.

Become a focus for all lovers in ME, and love will flow to you in abundance.

Ya azim.

Creation needs your free, open,
and courageous heart,
so that you can create a new Earth and a new
Heaven together with ME.

Stop the Insanity of Normality

Why continue to collaborate with what creates misery in both you and others?

Love begins with self-change.

Stop the insanity of normality.
Stop the massacre of human beings.
Stop the massacre of animals.
Stop the destruction of meadows, fields, forests, streams, lakes and oceans that were originally made for us to celebrate our feasts of love in.

Our new power begins when we step out of powerlessness.
All living beings have a right to life.
This planet was created as a home for all beings.
There are no boundaries and no private rights for the rich.

Stop the insanity of complicity.
We eat animals that were murdered in mass cages.
We lead lives of consumption for which millions of people are enslaved.

We choose perfumes to please our friend – and ignore the fact that animals were tormented and tortured to produce them.

The new fascism emerges from insidious indifference and powerlessness.

We can no longer be happy in such a world.

In the search for our lost happiness, we want to find international friendship and a family of the heart, that lives, acts and thinks for peace on this planet.

This great family is a family of plants, animals and humans.

Let us together step out of this eternal chain of complicity by daring to dream and act for a better world again.

We no longer allow ourselves to be talked into believing that we cannot achieve anything.

We no longer allow ourselves to be talked into believing that what is happening everywhere is meaningful.

We no longer allow ourselves to be talked into believing that conforming to this world serves any good.

We no longer allow ourselves to be talked into accepting society's ideas about profession and future.

We no longer allow ourselves to be drawn into the endless lies of society's double standards.

We no longer allow ourselves to be locked up in the prison of love relationships that are much too small, closing the doors to much larger possibilities of love in this world.

Let us step out of the private cages of love that is no love at all.
We take part in the global war by saying to the one we love: If you are unfaithful to me, I will kill you.

Let us step out of this insanity and the constant distrust of one another, for this can never result in a healing force for a positive revolution.
Love is free and leads us onto sure paths if we

follow it. Let us create places where we can trust the voice of our heart again. Let us find common songs, words and deeds that turn this world into a love affair.

Thank you and ya azim.

Let us create places where we can trust the voice of our heart again.

Longing and Fulfillment

Imagine waking up one morning and no longer having fear.
Imagine that you awaken, step out of your door, and hear the calling of a bird, as if it were the first time you heard it. You recognize its language, for it is your language, too.

Healing thoughts are born of an open heart.

You no longer need any old religion, ideology or moral appeals. Amazed, you realize to what extent religion was a bulwark against life itself.

Astonished, you realize how your atheism was a fight against a projected God. Now you can leave God alone, for God's sake.

Imagine that you are free of all that, because you are connected to the world of perception, fully connected with the divine world and its becoming.

You thankfully take on the responsibility of being a co-creator, by remaining connected with the creative spirit, the Spirit of the World, in all your thoughts and deeds.

You no longer need to moan and groan, pray and hope for things that you cannot believe will be fulfilled. Now you know that there is thirst because there is also water.

You know that there is fulfillment of your longing if you connect with it fully and recognize it fully.

You should know that your longing is unique and can only be fully recognized by you. As long as you see others' longing as your own, you cannot find fulfillment, and you will remain separated.

As long as you carry the knowledge of others as protection against yourself and spread it as an ideology, there can be no peace. But you have begun to make your knowledge into your knowledge. Your life has become your prayer.

You have now fully stepped out of comparison and turned your own longing into your voice. Now you know that you have accepted joint responsibility for the overall work of Creation through your uniqueness.

At the same time you recognize your voice in everybody else.

You know that your own becoming, and thus the becoming of the world, speaks through your true longing.

You know that fulfillment is inherent in your longing, just like water is inherent in the one who thirsts.

You know that your longing is your source and your power of germination, which will unfold at the right time.

In your longing lies the original knowledge of your whole being.

Since you know this now, you have become calm, firm and clear. You keep your quiet germinating power clear and unclouded.
The kind of longing that wears you down and your

impatience have left you, and you can calmly listen to the answers that the world is giving you, day by day, to carry you securely toward your goal.

May your clear longing and the knowledge of its fulfillment be the umbilical cord for your will, connecting you with the Soul of the World, with ME, carrying you and protecting you from false religiousness, ideology, or premature contentment.

Your true and uncorrupted longing is the voice of your cosmic self, guiding you safely and giving birth to you as the gestalt that you are.

Ya azim.

You know that fulfillment is inherent in your longing,
just like water is inherent in the one who thirsts.

Not Judging

Snuggle into the new presence of this day. May these 24 hours of your life be your work of art.

Let the past be past and enter into the new presence.

Notice how when you change, the whole world around you changes.

If you identify with the pain of the past, you connect with a determined future that brings sorrow and pain.

If you no longer hold on to pain, and if it has cleansed you because you have taken in the insight that it holds, you can begin to dance in the freedom of a new Creation.

Give the day back its shining with your light and your shining.

Do not become a scavenger of life energy by refusing to go with the changes that need to happen and by becoming a sucker of light. You are here to take

Not Judging

your light out into the world. Feel the millions of light particles that dance all around you and that want to manifest within you as the power of transformation into new states of being.

If you are facing difficulties, do the following:
Immerse yourself into the stillness of your heart and ask yourself: how can I best act here?

Open up to the frequency in which your inner voice is free of fears and doubts, and then act on the answer that you get.

In everything that you do, keep a loving connection to your friends. Do not enumerate their faults.

With every fault that you enumerate without providing them with a bridge for change, you build the walls of the cage of an everyday relationship, in which it will be difficult to fly.

With every fault that you only enumerate, you strengthen their fixation on their faults and tie them to them. Before judging another, try for a few minutes to see with his eyes, to feel with his feelings,

79

and think with his mind. It is then easier for you to connect to a possible solution that lies prepared for him in his situation.

Rise up like the Phoenix from the ashes and show him the next steps that he can take, if he is ready to leave his mistakes behind.

Give him some of the power and humor of self-change.

Simply naming faults does not contain any power of change.

But maybe you can see the inner beauty and entelechy of the other. As soon as he himself feels this beauty, the self-healing forces of entelechy are at work.

Whenever you have a tendency to react with personal emotions, think about the fact that there is a different way. Difficulties are overcome through ease.

Accept your own faults: Yes, that is how I am. It is only this acceptance that can free up the power of change. My faults, too, serve my development through the insights that I get from them.

If the noble one recognizes his faults, he gets rid of them.

Do not hold on to inner dialogues about yourself and others. It is absurd to complain that you are not seen or recognized for whom you are. Rectify your own mirror image, so that the world can see your true shining again.

You recognize the power of true readiness to change by the great cheerfulness that it brings. Oh, that's how I am!

Now you are ready to leave behind what you do not want to be.

Now you can leave the faults behind like a second skin that no longer fits you.

Once you have accepted something fully, you are no longer its victim. You can take on the responsibility.

Ya azim.

You recognize the power of true readiness to change by the great cheerfulness that it brings.

Remain Connected

Remain connected in everything you do. It is only when you begin to separate in your judgment, when you count ME out from certain thoughts and deeds, when you feel that there is no space for the divine power, this is when things in you get dammed up and become dark and evil. This is when a great power in you begins to rage and roil. It is without control, for you have taken away its divine guiding power of direction. Give ME space in those areas that you think are godless.

War is a result of energies that have been held back for a long time.

War is a result of you regarding your soul as bad, judging it, and therefore constantly keeping this part of your power from the world until it erupts independently and destructively.

The greatest dam in life is built of fear.

It is up to you to decide if MY becoming can work through you now. Your attention determines if the guided power of Creation can work through you. If you look at a wilting leaf – do you see death or life? If you look at a caterpillar that is weaving its cocoon – do you see death or life? If you look at a human being who is dying, do you see death or life?

Make yourself empty like a stone. Then MY focused power of creation of abundance can enter into you. **Leave fear behind. That is a decision.**

Even in the midst of the greatest destruction, which is not my will, MY healing power lies prepared.

May your will be done, may your will become MY will. Let MY will become your will.

Step out of the madness of false power, fear and separation.

Separation is an illusion. Do not take these words as consolation, but make them into your insight. Make them yours in all events and all things that you encounter. Love is an insight.
Your will and MY will become identical at the deepest level of the soul.

84

Know that MY will is life and not death.
MY will is love and not separation.
MY will is power and not fear.

Long live the power of evolution, renewal, beauty, youth, wisdom and age that have found their anchor and their foundation in love.

Ya azim.

> *Leave fear behind.*
> *That is a decision.*

The Power of Connection

You ask ME why it is always so difficult to stay with ME. Are you prepared to be still and hear the unusual answer?

The full answer requires that you enter into an unusually present state of being. That is one of the difficulties.

The place of the greatest difficulty for you is also the place of the greatest difficulty for ME. In this sense, the divine world always holds up a mirror to your self.

You will ask: Is then God so powerless? Does he not have the power to take me out of my despair or put me back on course if I have gotten lost?

Yes, the divine world has so little power over you, if you do not draw it to you. But it has full power if you are fully connected to it.

I cannot operate in you fully until you have been fully born, and that means fully discovering and

accepting ME and letting ME work fully through you.
It means that you recognize and accept the authority
you have through ME, also in difficult situations.
It occurs when your connection to ME has been
reestablished.

**The reason for the difficulty is usually that, when
you are in difficult situations, you seldom find the
stillness and depth necessary to hear me fully.
You then vibrate at a different frequency, where
everything seems to be infinitely difficult.**

It is especially difficult for you when you have
become entangled in private, personal ideas of love
and react with personal desire or are personally
offended.

It is easier if you remain connected to ME, also in
the midst of the difficulties and if you earnestly seek
ME.

Base your trust as deeply as you can in ME. I am
here and want to pave a way for you to walk with ME.
If you understand this step of trust, it will constantly
become easier.

Your path is easiest and most shining when you fully remember ME and when your trust becomes so deep that you recognize ME at the bottom of your soul.
Your body and your spirit are longing for this new shift of frequency in you.

Sometimes your body chooses an illness in order to lead your mind to a new insight and to prepare your body for the frequency that is necessary to meet the new.

Once you find this new level of frequency within you, then ease and playfulness enter into your life and into everything you do.
A deep and knowing sense of humor comes to you. Compassion and a great divine seriousness come to you.

This is the first step: Seek ME, also in your difficulties, and know that I am there. You can find ME also when it seems as if God has forsaken you.

Bring your mind and your body into a state of elasticity, so that there is space for ME within

you. At first that is a daily exercise; after a while it becomes natural.

Yes, remain with ME, even in your difficult moments. The gifts that you then find through ME and with ME are great.

I greet you and your faithfulness.
Ya azim.

Once you find this new level of frequency within you,
then ease and playfulness enter into your life
and into everything you do.
A deep and knowing sense of humor comes to

Words of the Goddess

In every woman there is an aspect of the Goddess that calls out and wants to come alive and blossom again.

How can the male God, whom you have honored and called upon for millennia, develop his love when you yourselves have constantly suppressed and killed his female side? You have taken love away from your God, and this can only lead to a cruel reality.

But I am deeply feminine.
You will find me in everything that lives, crawls, hears, smells, sings, tastes, chirps, breathes, shines and squeals.

It is absurd to regard this part of Creation as lowly, inferior or even devilish.

Those who seek God only in the beyond kill material life and thereby the Goddess.

I am the Soul of Nature, giving life to the Universe.

You men, when you touch the breast of a woman in natural lust, how often do you then realize that an aspect of the Goddess is revealing herself?

When you do your work, do you still think of the fact that you are cooperating with the Goddess herself and that you can listen to MY voice, MY will, MY longing and MY advice?

I am life in matter. Matter is not something "objective" that is separate from you. It is equally full of a subjective will and longing as you are.

Connect yourself firmly with MY presence. **MY pulse is here, immediately, within you.**

You will find ME in a pig, in a cuckoo, in the gaze of your neighbor, in your girlfriend, in a cricket or in a praying mantis. MY world calls out to you in everything and has a message for you.

The call of a toad, the croaking of a frog, two pigs that wallow in mud, the challenging eyes of a whore are not showing you anything base that one must avoid, which even Francis of Assisi believed.

Maybe they mirror a part of your longing and desire that you see as base in yourself and that calls out to be elevated and heard.

If you reconnect with MY simple and elementary voice, you will all by yourself become a messenger of the Goddess, a fighter for peace.
You will connect with MY compassion and no longer allow that the female voice is silenced.

With this mandate you will not want to tie any man to you, for you know that you thereby nourish his hatred and turn him into a warrior who will eventually kill the Goddess.
You will seek and find your fulfillment and your confirmation in ME and you will therefore no longer need acknowledgement and false proof of love from the outside.

You will stand up for true friendship between women, which does not fall apart if two women love the same man.

You will again take on your divine challenge and become an anchor and an orientation for men. With you and through you they will experience and get to know what a woman truly loves and what she does not love. You will see to it that they become servants of the Goddess.

Of course your voice will take a stand. It will take a stand for love and for all beings on this earth.

You will help to enable men to renew themselves by seeing MY presence in you and to become sensual lovers who love MY radiance.

You will help them lose their fear of ME, and you will help them serve ME through their love of you and your inner being.

It is through your joint unconditional love that the song of the earth can resound as it has never resounded before. That the streams, valleys, rivers, mountains and lakes can become the celebration that I am.

May MY longing and hope also be your longing and hope.

It is ME myself, whom you will receive when your longing has found peace.

Ya azim.

It is ME myself, whom you will receive when your longing has found peace.

The Beginning of Spring

A day of spring. A day when the morning is young; a day for setting off anew.
The new era can be inaugurated with you and with many other peace-bringers on earth. The time has come for an historic shift.

When the first human beings carry a true longing for peace within them, they will find it.

When you long to do what is right and to walk the right path, you will.

The transition to a new era wants to be understood and initiated as deeply and thoroughly as possible.

The path of political action is a path of self-knowledge.

You live under exceptional circumstances. You have access to exceptional gifts of abundance.
Only few people on earth live the way you do and have the possibility of seeing, understanding, and acting.

Enter into compassion, but do not let yourselves be broken by it.

Those who are here to initiate a new historic state of peace need the strength to focus on and see what is happening on earth.
But they also need the power and the intelligence to realize what new possibilities they here hold in their hands.

Become aware of the infinitely abundant possibilities for your fulfillment.
Peace is a result of consciously accepting abundance.

Do not be afraid of the magnitude of the task. And do not see the work as being connected to effort and pain.

Enter into the waters that take you safely to your goal. The new political morning is born of the power of the joy of life and of insight.

Caring for your health and welfare are prerequisites for keeping your mind open and for participating in the fate of the world. They thus become a kind of inner duty.

The new revolution takes place quietly. It wants to be born of the ability to have joy in life and to perceive. It takes place within you at the speed that comes naturally to you, when you no longer have to hide from the eyes of others.

Find your own protection by fully connecting with trust. Do not teach and convince others by placing yourselves above them.

The desire to convince others has led to the violation and destruction of many other forms of existence. Instead, follow the path of inner truth and perception. Stand for what you are convinced of, without being afraid of the eyes of others. Stand for it simply and clearly. A compassion that is born of perception is convincing of itself.

Committed seekers who walk their own path create a field that has an impact. An opened heart is always contagious. A loving erotic energy that comes from the heart and is free of fear creates

a great magnetic force field around it. This force field enables many new powers and forms to enter into reality and create history.

Ya azim.

> *The new political morning*
> *is born of the power of the joy of life*
> *and of insight.*

The Goddess' Prayer

I greet this morning and invite the Goddess to assemble within me. I invite the spirit of universal love to see through my eyes, to become aware, and to act through my hands. I invite the Goddess of sensual love to realize herself in my body and through my actions. I invite the spirit of love in all its aspects, so that I can see and understand its inner laws through my eyes.

I am who I will become.

I give thanks for this infinite possibility.

I fill myself with the stability and emptiness that makes it possible for me to be still in YOU. I fill myself with the spirit of trust, which makes it possible for me to see with YOUR eyes.

My cells fill up with YOUR divine light. They are dancing and celebrating in YOU. They are quivering in anticipation of approaching a new Creation together with YOU. May the age of partnership and of sensual love begin.

"It was as if the sky had quietly kissed the earth,
so that in a shower of blossoms she must only
dream of him."

May the call of the bird be YOUR morning greeting
to me. The landscape of the Goddess stretches
out toward me and fills my body with a new quiet
certainty of YOUR presence.

What better future on this earth than the full
presence of **YOUR bodily and knowing life?** May
my bodily existence be fulfilled through YOUR
bodily existence.
**I thank YOU Goddess, Mother Earth, for being
present in me and in all beings with your physical,
natural, sensual and sexual presence.**

We wish to touch YOUR spirit and YOUR body in
everything that YOU are.

Help us to hear, see, and understand YOUR
language and YOUR presence.

Put the memory back in our cells that we have come
in order to realize YOUR paradise on earth.

We want to understand all aspects of what it means to live and love on earth in the full awareness and presence for each other and for YOUR work.

THY kingdom come, THINE will and THINE celebration be done – here with us and over the whole earth.

I greet the rain and the sparrows in front of my hut.
Ya azim.

I invite the Goddess of sensual love
to realize herself in my body
and through my actions.

What Can I Do?

The easier you can enter into the maze of time and difference, without losing sight of the whole, the more encompassing is the power of change that can operate within you. More encompassing information can at every moment be accessed in the global destruction and in the fear. Information of peace vibrates at the more encompassing level. It is at the more encompassing level that you can access what you need, also in difficult situations.

When you clear away your last inner bulwark, when the divine soul of the world can look through the eyes of human beings even in the midst of personal or global crises, and when the human being does not close his eyes, then MY power of new creation can have an infinite effect.

Connect with ME in your heart, even in difficult situations.
Let the whole, the divine light, shine into all your details. **For it is especially in the most difficult situations that I want to be discovered and recognized.**

What you can do?
Strive for MY perfection at every moment.

It may at first seem complicated and difficult, for after all, there is a habit on earth that is thousands of years old to suppress ME from the history of the human being and seek ME where I am not. Let ME see with your eyes, even in the most difficult situations. Do not shut off your eyes from MINE.

The power that provides answers and creates fields can then be realized through you and through your type of perception. It is a process of field creation. You are entering the vibration, you are preparing it. The more people consciously act at this preparatory level, the more powerfully can the power of transition take effect.

This leads to a historic point of transition. **The new frequency can take hold on earth, vibrate in it and with it, and operate as a field-creating and history-creating power in everything.**

The power of a mighty, vital, sensual and creative peace can manifest itself.

103

This is not achieved through effort. There is much too much to do for you to be able to achieve it on your own power.

It suffices for you to make an effort to perceive ME, also in difficult situations. The rest can then happen by itself.

Ya azim.

> *Let ME see with your eyes,*
> *even in the most difficult situations.*
> *Do not shut off your eyes from MINE.*

Connect with MY Dream

Connect with MY dream, which is also yours, and let new creation arise from this process.

MY dream also lives in nature and in the landscape that surrounds you. You can connect with this dream and then realize it in gardening and ecology.

You recognize if you are connected with MY dream by your gain in power. Being connected with the dream of Creation always leads to a gain in power.

It is only when the connection with MY dream, the dream of the Soul of Creation, is lost that the feeling arises of having to act from your own effort and to possibly stand alone against a whole world.

The dream of community is dreaming itself through you.

Through you the dream of a universal society and the connectedness with all existence is dreamt.

Connected with ME, you no longer need to protect yourselves and isolate yourselves from a strange world. You learn what it means to be protected through an aware presence and connectedness.

Connected with ME, you will no longer think in categories of possessions. Everything that you have is with you, so that you recognize and redeem the inner dream through your realization.

Ya azim

*The connection with the dream of Creation
always leads to a gain in power.*

The Dream of the Children

Give your children the possibility to connect with their dream.

You will no longer think: these are my children, they belong to me. All children are the children of Creation, they come from ME and return to ME. They come with their own plan for life.

It is possible that you will find in your children your cosmic companions and teachers.

Do not try to realize your own unfulfilled longings through your children. Realize them yourself.

Listen to the language of your children and sense their dream; this will awaken your own dream. Once you begin to see and understand their dream, children are a blessing for your own awakening.

Support them, so that their wisdom can come to them. They need your love, your strictness, your clarity, and your truth.

They especially need you to step out of relationship, so that they can remain free for their relationship with the world.

Connect with the dream of your children. This connection brings about a growth of power within you.

Essentially, it is you mothers who determine if your sons grow up to be jealous lovers and possessive monsters – or if they stand free with a loving, cosmic connection to the world.

Protect your children by giving them the freedom that is theirs. Give them enough time alone, so that they do not lose their connection. Protect them from the ping pong of relationships. See to it that they remain connected to the source from which they came – even in your presence. It will never be as easy as during these first years of life to learn to see and understand the spirit of plants, animals and angels.

Protect this sacred space of the children by becoming aware of this connection with

Creation. Do not disturb them if they happen to be connected with Creation as they dream awake. Instead, use this for your own reconnection.

Children have their own angels, their guides, and companions. Accompany them on this journey of awareness, meditative stillness, and communication. Become their companions, too, and help them find orientation.

Do not be alarmed if they temporarily reveal themselves as revolting little monsters. They are briefly repeating the entire process of human evolution and history. Give them clear orientation here, too, based on your own power of stillness.
Give your children the opportunity to find and accept their cosmic being.

*Listen to the language of your children
and sense their dream;
this will awaken your own dream.*

The Great Power of Change

Now is an especially good time for the emergence and realization of new thoughts. Stay awake, so that the spiritual family that will make it possible to prepare and initiate the new age can find itself.
News of horrors will continue to spread over the globe, for the powers of destruction are still in charge.

Watch what is happening, but do not let yourselves be carried away by it. Parallel to this, the new powerful networks of the heart and a new process of realization are emerging.

A great power of change is setting in.

Not least is it due to the own inner work that you are doing that more and more healing powers can enter and take effect on earth.

Remain stable and clear when creating a vision for the age of a new global peace. Learn to integrate the tremendous elementary powers into your vision of peace.

This work can dissolve many old karmic patterns; it is like a process of inner cleansing and clarification.

Do not follow the horrors of the past. A new presence and a new possibility for fulfillment want to be understood and accessed by you. I am with you. Ya azim.

Learn to integrate the tremendous elementary powers into your vision of peace.

Find Peace and Calm Within

Open up, become Light, for your Light comes.
Cleanse yourself daily with the question: Do I want
to become a messenger of a new peace? Take time
to enter the day with this conscious decision.

Many people belittle those who seriously ask
themselves if this world can yet be saved. To be an
"idealist" has become a dirty world.

**Do not see through the judging eyes of others,
but connect with MY eyes and MY seeing. It is
the eyes of a new creation.**

If you now go into the world with a newly won inner
freedom, the eyes of others will no longer be able to
throw you off your center.

The peace that has the power of realization must first
of all be found within. You find it by becoming aware
of MY presence within you. Seek the protective
space of MY great inner peace, time and again. It
holds the protection that you need and the answers
that are the right ones for you, right now.

You thereby pave the way for others to go through this great inner gate, behind which new, never seen revelations are waiting for you.

God, the Soul of the World, lies within. It lies in you and in all things. There, you can call upon its beauty, wisdom, and inner calm.

Home is not only where your friends are. Home is everywhere, when you remain connected to ME, also in the presence of others.

Make yourself the focal point of all true seekers by remaining faithful to your seeking, also in the presence of others.

May the place where you live and work become a spiritual school of life, where you can learn the inner wisdom of life that enables you to see, call forth and realize this inner peace everywhere in the world.

Time is short. There is no more time for ego games. Specifically because time is so short, you should take the time and the peace and quiet to listen to MY inner voice within you. Therefore, follow MY calling within you and become the power of realization that you are.

Dare to connect with ME totally. For I am the world soul of nature that gives life to the universe.

Time is so short that the first priority is to seek out the power of calm that gives you the strength to act in such a way that you connect with love and trust. It is through this inner decision that your excessive anger can be anchored in sacred rage. This gives you the courage needed for self-change and for taking action.

Trust is not something that is simply there of itself. It is an active determination that carries a new power of realization within it. It is an inner decision.

Through this inner decision you stop blaming others and you take on your own responsibility.

You, who want to know ME:
Know that your longing and your seeking do not change anything unless you know the following secret: If you do not find within you what you are seeking, then you will not find it anywhere else.

Know that from the beginning it was I, and it is I, whom you will receive when your wants and desires come to rest.

From this inner connection you will find the source of the contact, perception and action that is needed in every moment.

Ya azim.

> *If you do not find within you*
> *what you are seeking,*
> *then you will not find it anywhere else.*

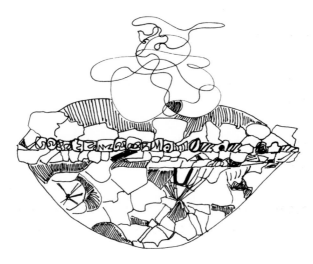

The Artist's Task

I ask the power of universal Love to give me presence and clarity for this day. I connect with the eye of a new seeing. I ask for messages on the subject of art in our time.

Art is not based on ability. Art comes from the encounter with true, unprejudiced seeing. In this sense, the artist is a true Zen master.
It is good if you understand your trade, but that is not yet art. May your trade be your power tool, helping you to walk the path of art.

Art comes from a deep connection with the world of Creation. It comes from the inner willingness to let go of the old again and again, opening up to something new.

True art is always a new birth. You take part in the aspect of the "I" of the world in which the world always consists of new creation.

Art is not a question of ability in the traditional sense of the word, but it comes from the inner willingness of the learner to keep his/her inner seeing eye so open that it sees and perceives the new every day. **That is the great and true ability of an artist, which lies beyond any fashion or taste.**

Art is always a new birth. Be prepared. The rest happens all by itself. Do not be concerned with your skillfulness. It comes all by itself, as soon as you let go and understand how to go with and be what you perceive.

Do what you do, fully. Do it consciously and clearly; then you will rise above the fog of naturalism and notice that the world is never what you thought it to be.

Use humor to destroy your many old ideas and images of what the world is supposed to be, until the child-like awe and joy of doing brings you back to yourself. Art is the celebration of Creation. Art is devotion and sanctification. Art is the deepest connection with pure beingness, without any further intent or goal.

Whenever you truly become an artist, you will be lifted up to a level of insight, which lets you see and understand the connections of true peace much deeper. In this sense, art always also means working on oneself. The result is the true life artist.

The result is a person who with amusing calm has integrated the many aspects of beingness as a creator. A deep reconciliation occurs with oneself and with the world, and this reconciliation can bring forth true change.

An artist is no longer a victim, neither of himself, nor of the world.
From this connectedness you will take back the true joy of life in the simplest aspects of your everyday life. This joy of life is deeper and quieter than the first jubilation that was there in the beginning.

You have never seen the world deeper, even in its pain, suffering and unresolved aspects. Here, you no longer identify with the role of a victim.

You have recognized the celebration that you experience when you take in the aspects of the world through the eyes of art. That is the "ecstatic Yes" that Friedrich Nietzsche knew.

New icons will emerge from the new creative spirit of art, and they will have a deeper peace-creating effect than all appeals and all political speeches that come from the point of view of everyday life.

I greet you. Ya azim.

Use humor to destroy your many old ideas and images of what the world is supposed to be, until the child-like awe and joy of doing brings you back to yourself.

To All Peace Workers

Human beings have been praying for peace for millennia and they have fought for peace, but in their inner consciousness they have forgotten what peace is.
They no longer know its inner laws.

Human beings lack an encompassing inner vision of peace.

A vision is an objective reality that can be seen and felt from within. It is inherent as a possibility in evolution and is waiting to be seen and accessed by humans again.

Peace is a question of the frequency of consciousness.

At the divine level of consciousness, peace is simply there in an elementary way.

The Divine is always simple, everything else is complicated. To connect with this simplicity seems to be the most difficult thing for humans to do.

Human peace has not been realized yet, because it is not known as a vision on a collective consciousness level.

True peace is not wishful thinking and not an escape into a dream world; true peace can only be realized when one has begun to see and understand in a comprehensive way.

Peace is much more than the opposite of fighting and much more than the opposite of war.

Peace is manifested new consciousness.

True peace always begins within. It cannot be realized without full inner transformation.

This is where the mistake and the insanity lies among so many peace fighters, who want to ignore this fact.

They seek an external peace without understanding anything about the inner connections.

Their fight for peace is an escape from themselves. Countless wars and infinite destruction have resulted from the insanity of fanatic fights for peace. Peace cannot come about by trying to force certain morals or a world view on others. Peace is a quality of existence and has nothing to do with world views.

Peace does not mean renunciation, for renunciation often results in inner dissatisfaction.

Peace can best grow from the fullness of a life that is fully lived. Before that you will always go in circles around yourself.

Peace can only be realized when your wishes, longing and desire have become still.

The yogi comes to the conclusion that he must renounce the world. But that is usually also a form of escape.

The world was created in its abundance so that peace can be seen as the abundance of its richness and its joy.

Divine consciousness does not create any needs in order for you to renounce them. It also does not create any needs in order for you to succumb to them.

Every true need, every wish, and every longing is your teacher and serves a higher insight.

When you see that, you enter into a new level of apprenticeship.

Every inner desire is your signpost to God.

Peace can only be realized by again trusting that an answer or a fulfillment, which is already inherent in the real wish, can be realized.

This trust is a decision.

Quiet and determined, you set off toward new shores. Your inner voice guides you on your way.

You go into the world as a student, in order to learn something new from every experience. It is specifically this attitude that makes you awake and alive and makes you a teacher for others.

You will be guided naturally to those places and focal points of the world where your inner light can shine. Your surroundings will change through your inner decision.

Create places where the inner connections of peace can be understood and seen.

That is the greatest deed that the world needs most
urgently right now.

Thank you and amen.

> *The Divine is always simple;*
> *everything else is complicated.*

God, why do YOU allow all this to happen?

How is it possible that children die?

How is it possible that 6000 women are cruelly circumcised every day in Africa?

How is what happened in Kosovo, Rwanda, in Vietnam and Auschwitz possible?

How am I to believe in YOU, when I see what is happening on earth, without anyone trying to truly prevent it?

How am I to believe that prayers change anything when most people still follow the religions of power?

How can YOU remain so still, why are you so inaudible and so ineffective, if you are a God of Love?

Goddess, if YOU exist somewhere, in the universe or in our hearts, why do YOU not give us more power?

How is it possible for the world to be the way it is?

Why could YOU never intervene, when atrocities occurred?

In Creation, the human being was given the freedom of choice. Wherever the human being chooses against ME, the Divine has no power.

But now time has become short. It is not the wish of Creation to leave the world to the destructive forces. There is a connectedness with the divine love, which is higher than all violence. Today, the task is to realize it with ME.

If you, too, place yourself on the side of doubt and powerlessness, the chance of realizing a humane divine soul on earth diminishes greatly. You then deprive yourselves and ME of a large part of our free power to act.

There is no humane God without human beings.
There are no humane human beings without God.
God and the human being are inseparably connected to each other. Removing the illusion of separation, which results in an infinite amount of pain and destruction, is the topic of the times and of your work.

Who is speaking now? You or I? God or human being? I can only speak through you in this way, if you open up completely. The process of this speaking, the process of opening, occurs from you and from your willingness. It is your very own deepest decision to do this. In this sense, we are inseparably connected to each other.

There is only one existence, there is only one love, there is only one becoming. Life will continue eternally. For human beings the hour of a deep decision, an historical decision, is approaching.

Most people have lost their way so completely, that hardly anyone still remembers the true divine power that resides in human beings. Most people must first experience a very deep helplessness, in order to rediscover and acknowledge this power that comes from the connectedness with the divine power of creating.

This is the point that will lead some of you to a very high energy: there is a power for you that comes from your connectedness with the divine power of Creation. Creation, and the creation of the new world, occur through this connectedness.

Wherever men and women come together in this connectedness, they experience the joy of Creation. They feel the connectedness with a power that stands above all other powers. They create the new experience of Eros.

God is calling to human beings. Raise your voice and seek with ME those people who are willing to take the responsibility that arises by taking part in the destiny of the world.

You do not have to refer to MY name. So much wrong has been done in MY name.

Focus on your own true name. Wherever you are, act sincerely, creatively, truthfully, and out of love. Reconnect with your higher self, which knows and wants to realize your divine voice. Then you will receive the power to act in the name of peace.

Remember paradise – and realize it, wherever you can.

I greet you. Ya azim.

There is no humane God without human beings.

God is Powerless without Human Beings

I am not the power of destruction and death. I am love and everlasting life. I am this, also in the hour of death for those who live in connectedness with ME.

It is human beings who kill and oppress each other. It is human beings who have created the fear and the distrust. It is they who are exploiting and destroying the world; it is not I.

In Creation, human beings were given the freedom to be as God. This goes much deeper than you think. Here also lies the freedom to take a stand against Creation and against the Divine.
Whenever the human being decides against ME, the Divine has no power. But then life has no chance. The true power of survival exists only in the connectedness with ME.

Sooner or later every living being will return to ME, for there is no other possibility to survive.
No country will be able to survive without the true connectedness of the below with the above, of earth with heaven, of human being with God.

The pain I feel about the situation on earth is not less than yours. Never before has the Goddess called so intensely to humans to reawaken and rediscover and accept their connectedness with ME.

A new power of change will emerge from a universal connectedness that has freed itself from false morals and religiousness. It has the power to initiate the birth of new cultures.

A new power to act will arise from this connectedness. A new language, the language of universal love, can then be spoken and understood again.

When human beings connect to their divine origins, the divine source regains the authority of its peace-creating power.

This is an essential act by the human being, an act that the world has been waiting for, for so long.

You do have to accept that you are of a divine nature.

Ya azim.

> *A new power to act will arise -*
> *from this connectedness.*

Trust is the Key to the New World

Stretch out your senses towards the world and open them to this day. Connect your body and your mind with MY source, which is moving toward a new future.

Without your active participation, the longed-for future cannot come about. You therefore need ME and MY power, so that you can always nourish yourself from it.

You yourselves are like the blade of grass under a layer of concrete that cries out for new life.

The entire knowledge that is needed for the new age lies like a key inside of you, in your entelechy, as a prehistoric memory.

This source lies within you, and it is inexhaustible. But as long as it remains forgotten, it can unfold only a little. It cannot take effect fully in you until you have found a deep trust in its effectiveness again.
It is only in a state of full trust that this source can be seen in its entirety. Rebuilding trust is the

key for the emergence of a peaceful world. Find this basic trust again.

It is as if this channel opens up an entirely different holographic world view for you.

Taking the step of fully trusting the healing powers of life itself is the same as taking the step into enlightenment.

Do not let yourselves be thrown off this path of trust when you look into the world with empathy and see all the horrific things that occur. On the surface, there is little cause for hope.

Your empathy threatens to pull you into intense despair, hopelessness and powerlessness. Or else a protective layer of indifference is created, which no longer makes it possible to connect with the healing source. Retain your empathy and still retain your trust.

Understand the words: not on your own power.

Imagine that a seedling had to ask itself if it is able to push through a layer of asphalt. It is protected by not knowing this question. It follows the power of its inner goal and entelechy.

Here, you will find the theology of decision.

The divine source needs the full power of your trust, so that you focus on and follow the simplest and truest values of life and love.

All by itself, this leads you to a life and love that is full of sensuality and empathy.

Then, a truth can begin to operate in your bodies and your minds that has been forgotten and suppressed for thousands of years.

Here lies the greatest doubt, for it does not seem possible to make this decision. You always reach the limits of habitual fears.

But in the decision to trust lies the protection against fear and violence.

Here lies the healing power that connects you permanently with your deeper purpose.

Make the place where you live and work into an oasis, where you can practice this trust in the universal healing power of life.

Make the place where you live into a school for the creation of trust, so that you get to know and understand its prerequisites.

This will lead you to a new study of life itself and opens up a new pathway of knowledge for you to your own library of life and love.

It is only through this decision that your inner seminal power can be set free.

It is only through this decision that the principle of field creation for peace can take full effect.

In the name of Eros and community, in the name of the original source, for a life on this planet that is lived to the fullest extent.

Ya azim.

The divine source needs the full power of your
trust,
so that you focus on and follow
the simplest and truest values of life and love.

Sensual Love Needs to be Anchored in the Universe

I connect with the divine presence.

I greet the light of this day, I connect with the beauty of the universal promise, and I give thanks for the possibility of being here.

There is a yearning in the world, a sensuous longing, which fills my body with knowledge, for it is full of memories of the cosmic dream. All souls take part in this dream.
There is a cosmic dream that gives me protection and security, for it places me in a greater context.
There is a conviction that can liberate me from my restlessness, my powerlessness, and my feeling that all longing is in vain.
There is a love that is higher than all violence, for it is connected to certainty. Working on a new image of love is to create this certainty.

Within me, I hear the Goddess say:
Once you have found the great love toward the universal mother again, once you have found security

in her universal body, which always welcomes your arrival, then you have found the home of every love. Then you have found your anchor again, which can carry all earthly love relationships on their earthly plane.

Then you no longer need to seek in your love partner what you did not find in your mother. **You no longer need to seek in a single person what you have lost in the Universe.**

The tragedy of the love relationships of the last centuries is that something is being sought where it cannot be found.

You have a difficult history behind you.
The cosmic umbilical cord, which was connected to Nammu, the original mother, and which accompanied every personal dream of love, has been severed. This constantly leads you to the tragedy of unfulfilled love relationships.

It is only by reconnecting to Nammu, in the deep security of the universe, that the power is found that can calm the fear of loss.

The pain that is represented through Oedipus can only exist because the cosmic connection was lost.

Every erotic love can only gain permanence if its anchor in the Universe has been found again.

Ultimately, every true love relationship is of a universal nature. It is always a cosmic dream of love that is dreamed by two people. In this knowledge and in this connectedness they will manifest the personal love that up to now they had driven away through a much too narrow fixation on each other.

Learn to see yourself again in your eternal gestalt that now wants to realize a part of its cosmic dream of love on this earth.
This perspective brings peace to something inside of you. The universal connection and the re-connection with your sacred image give you peace and security.

Sometimes the pain of separation must go very far before the mistake in love is acknowledged and the new path toward spiritual connectedness is taken.
In the face of death, at the very latest, you sense

the cosmic secret that lies behind every true love relationship.

The soul has a hunger that cannot be stilled on the earthly level alone. It always extends into an invisible but larger world and it can only be pacified at that level.

Without this, every love relationship leads to the insanity of unfulfilled longing, because you are seeking fulfillment where it cannot be found.

Behind every desire, every sensual craving, and every erotic longing there is a cosmic longing and a cosmic promise of home.

When you have rediscovered this deep foundation within, you know the goal of your longing. This insight brings peace to something inside of you, and your body begins to be able to handle the great longing.

Now you are in a position to enter into the cosmic, sensual play of love and the dance of erotic power, because you have found the source with which to handle the erotic dance.

From this source, you can realize the dream of love on earth, for the pattern needed for this, the entelechy, reside fully within you. This eternal presence of the original mother is waiting and longing for you to find and acknowledge it again.

Here, the earth is dreaming its cosmic, earthly dream of love with you and through you. It is the eternal dream of the sexes.

Thank you and amen!

Behind every desire, every sensual craving,
and every erotic longing
there is a cosmic longing
and a cosmic promise of home.

The Power of Great Presence

The sparrows are romping around on the roof. The sun has already risen. The mind also wants to romp around from one place to another. Use this early morning hour for the power of presence and awareness. Every day it holds a new treasure for you, a treasure that you can experience so intimately only once.

Presence is connection.

That is the gift and the power of every true meditation. Become a witness of the dynamics inherent in the power of presence.

You do not need to believe in a God or Goddess to come to the source of presence, where you can see how realities are created from the state of great presence.

This is the great art of true yogis. They acquire this power through the art of renouncing the world. But you can use this source to turn toward the things of this world from the state of presence.

Empty yourself and become a witness of how your body and your cells fill up with light. This emptiness is the beginning of every true new creation. Feel how peace flows into you immediately and how the universal source of unconditional beauty wants to gather in you in celebration.

This is a universal beauty and power, which suffuses the entire earth with its soul, and which can speak to you as a quiet revelation.
It is the soul that touches you as a quiet play of light in the Portuguese summer or that calls you through the scent of an apple blossom.

That, which calls you externally with its magnetic beauty, wants to gather in you and become a creative force in the temple of your soul.

In this quiet greeting, which comes from presence, you have assembled much world inside of you. In this greeting, your mind and spirit automatically experience the expansion and growth that they desire for the day. It is solely in the power of presence and awareness that things gain their sacredness and their special presence.

If you look at the things and the people that you love from this state of presence, you no longer need to chase after them. It is simply by being perceived that they regain the beauty and the respect that they need to remain beautiful and universal for you.

It is through this process that the magic of attraction occurs.

The inner magic of beauty itself comes from presence, awareness, and consciousness. It brings forth universal faithfulness, and it has the necessary strength to manifest the faithfulness.

This process automatically gives things the right distance and closeness that make erotic fulfillment possible. New creation is achieved in this way.

It is the power of presence and awareness that makes it possible for you to recognize yourself as a source of creation and to transform things with magical power.

You will break the spell that has bound you to your fear and that has always let you follow a

destiny that, unknowingly, you created yourself through your subconscious fear.

Because of the cosmic loss and the cosmic forgetting, you were under the spell of chasing after a love that you had lost in yourself.

You thought that fulfillment lies in finding the other. But this fulfillment is only possible if you yourself have again found the beauty that comes from inner presence.

Finding the power of awareness and presence within oneself again is an essential secret of love. It is the beginning of the fulfillment that you are seeking.

Ya azim.

That which calls you externally
with its magnetic beauty
wants to gather in you
and become a creative force
in the temple of your soul.

Build the Rhythm

You need a solid rhythm to build a force of peace. Forces vibrate in the universe. Rhythm creates resonance and attracts the power.

Everyone has a personal rhythm of their own, a community has a rhythm, there is a rhythm between lovers, and there is a cosmic rhythm.

The more a community finds the universal rhythm, the more power will flow toward it.

The more a community creates its universal rules to be simple and clear, the more the individual can find freedom within it.

The entire universe vibrates in a clear rhythm and with the highest precision.
Is it not a true miracle with what precision the sun, the earth and the moon complete their orbits?

The more stable the rhythm of a community has become, the more reliably can the individual take

his/her place in it, and the more pure mind will be available for the day.

See to it that this rhythm is strengthened like the pulse of an organism. Once you have achieved that, then you can also sometimes break the rhythm and allow a creative chaos to reign, without weakening the whole. Without the power of a solid rhythm, no growth can reach its great, universal goal.
Make it a habit to get up reliably every day and to find your shining – like the sun.

Open up to the world first, before you focus on yourself or on your problems.

Ya azim.

Without the power of a solid rhythm,
no growth can achieve its great, universal goal.

Take Care of Your New Inner Birth

When the day touches the night and the first rays of light brighten the young morning, then your inner light, too, reaches out toward new perfection.

Protect and take care of the consciousness of a new beginning, of that which is unborn, unsaid, and undone within you, as you would an embryo that is soon to be born.

Focus your mind and spirit on this future within you.

The more awareness, presence and anticipation you can direct toward this birth process, the more powerful the new creation will be.

You are here because something new is growing within you. It has its own time and hour.

Be awake and precise.

Do not let your seedling whither unnoticed in you. It needs attention, care and presence to be able to unfold.

If you perceive it, then a powerful force of new creation is set free within you. Give attention and care to the contact. It is only in this way that it can unfold.

Connect with the spirit of the community, let the presence of the others and the mirrors that they give you spur you on in your own development. You can recognize yourself in their mirror.

A greater peace-creating Spirit wants to be realized through you. In this, your ego, your vanity, and your judgment and condemnation are of little importance. They only slow down the process of development in you and others.

The joint spirit of truth, participation, and solidarity with the power of change wants to unfold through you. In this, your inner power of germination plays a role that cannot be replaced.

Imagine that you are an organ in the overall organism, without which the whole cannot function. Your kidneys are not your liver and your heart is not your intestines.

It is only through the whole that each part unfolds and reaches fulfillment, and the whole could not function without its parts.

It is important for your inner healing that you realize which part in the whole you are, so that an overall healing can occur.

Give your inner power of germination to the world, for you are needed.
Give your true thoughts and actions to the world.
Give your serving and revolutionary power to the world, for you are needed.

When you give back your inner power of germination to the universe in full trust, your own healing can begin.
Take these steps of your new becoming every day anew – and you will receive back the entire power of growth of the universe as a gift.

I greet a whole universe in you.

I greet you as a part of the whole.

Ya azim.

*The more awareness, presence and anticipation
you can direct toward this birth process,
the more powerful will be the new creation.*

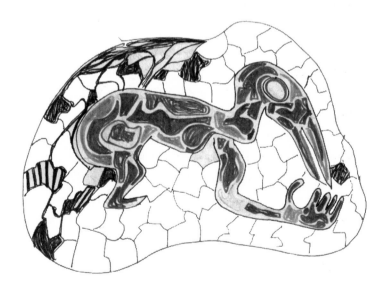

May My Life Be My Prayer

I connect with the power of universal love.
I call the peace-creating power to radiate within me and through me.
I invite the universal powers of consciousness to expand within me, so that its knowledge, power and insight may shine through me.

I let light and luminosity into my cells, that they may begin to dance in the light of eternal renewal.

My life is my prayer. I invite the power of universal love to unfold in me and through me.
May my body be a temple of divine love.
May my body be a temple of the Goddess.
May my body be a temple of sensual love in celebration of her.

May my life be in praise of earthly existence.
I give thanks that I may be here, now, at this time, with its calling and urging for change – that we finally may become knowing and can take on the human responsibility of becoming guardians of peace for this earth.

May my thoughts, words and deeds be powers of realization that make it possible for the desired peace to spread on this planet.

Let us together build this peace, wherein we again can learn to speak and understand the language of the Goddess, the language of the earth, the language of all creatures and the language of sensuality and contact.

May my longing be the messenger of YOUR peace. I call the gentle power, which is stronger than all violence: fill us entirely, give us the insight that makes it possible to end war on this earth.

Let us recognize the laws of inner peace so deeply that they become a part of us, so that we no longer flee from a cruel world into the beyond of artificial religions or into the false nests of a love that is much too small.

I call the majesty of universal love:
May YOUR love be my love.
May YOUR will be my will.
May YOUR alertness be my alertness.

May YOUR struggle be my struggle.
May YOUR insight be my insight.
May YOUR commitment be my commitment.
May YOUR power be my power.

I call upon the power of sacred rage:
Liberate us from our powerless personal anger, and fill us with the high energy that allows us to act fearlessly in every situation. May it again become possible for the humane power for all beings of the earth to be realized through us.

I connect with my higher self and ask it to give me the words that bring power, love and insight in these difficult times. I give thanks for YOUR power of infinite love, which never runs dry and I open all my senses, so that YOU may speak and work through me.

Thank you and amen.

May my life be my prayer.

The Source

Can you imagine a flourishing biotope that is separated from its source? Every flourishing garden lives from its source.

There is always nourishment at the root of this source. It does not increase, it does not decrease. There is no effort involved in making the garden flourish. It is only if the source is removed that life in the biotope withers, unless you feed it artificially.

A human being who wants to exclude the Soul of the World from his/her life is like a plant that separates itself from its source.
The ego comes into being, a piece of separated life that is removed from its source and now sees itself as the source.

The ego begins to run amok. For a while it has resources that it can feed on. But at some point they dry up, and it cannot find anything to feed on forever. It takes in artificial food that only makes it puff up. No artificial food contains the "Mana" of eternal life.

But the human being exists and lives in the face of eternity. **At some point, either in this lifetime or the next, it will have to return to the source, in order to survive. It will have to give up the antics with which it is trying to prove that it, too, is someone.**

Without the source, you cannot have permanence. Your life no longer has a meaning to give it its power and breath. When you are connected to the source you are whole – and you do not have to prove anything to anyone.

Once you are connected to the source, there is no effort and no boredom, no excessive laziness and no consuming busy-ness. You know when to be still and when to act. Your work is fulfilled through you with the greatest precision, for you are the work that wants to be fulfilled.

Your inner necessity is your driving force. Once you have let go of your ego's antics that tell you that this is too demanding, too trivial, too stupid or too difficult for you, you will be surprised at how precisely you know what must be done.

Your source knows what you need; follow it and drink from it. Nothing is demanded of you, that you cannot do. Your life gets its meaning and its original beauty through its connection with the source.

Ya azim.

> *Your source knows what you need;*
> *follow it and drink from it.*
> *Nothing is demanded of you, that you cannot*
> *do.*

The Now

May peace be with you and with your spirit.

May quiet sensuality fill your body in still presence for the moment.

The now is the source that wants to be perceived by you in an ever deeper and more encompassing way.

If you silence your concepts and ideas about what must be, then the presence of what is, begins.

You are astonished that anything exists at all. You are touched by the miracle of this existence, and that gives this day its own magic.

This source is so deep, so encompassing, so inexhaustible and healing, that it can transform you in every moment. It is present now and always.

The now is what holds the great miracle.
The now is that which always is and never dies.
The now is the source from which you can recover

the great miracle that gives you your shining through your presence.

You find the great secret that the eternity of Creation reveals itself in the essence and existence of the present.

You find no Creator behind it, no other substance. Existence itself gives Creation its permanence. It is eternal in its eternal power of transformation.

From the emptiness and liberation from all concepts, new Creation can emerge.
What is then born lives from the power of imagination and the will to realize that give things their limits and their form of appearance. Every reality comes from this source and lives from this freedom and its limitation.

Fill your body and your mind in this presence, and the miracle of Creation can flow through you and design its work through you.

True mastery, true healing power, and true love come from this presence of existence.

Introduce this secret also into all relationships that you want to care for. You thus give the others the freedom of a constant new creation.

Ya azim.

If you silence your concepts and ideas
about what must be,
then the presence of what is,
begins.

Fill up with Creation

Fill up with Creation.

Learn to see and understand the powers of Mana.
Perceive and use energy processes consciously for
your development.
Learn to understand the laws of happiness and joy.
**These are important contributions to the
emergence of a new culture and a new peace.**

Understand how awareness is focused, and when
exertion is needed. **Return to stillness again and
again.** For stillness is a starting point for new power
and new creation.

Become a witness. War almost always arises from
subconscious processes in you.

**Much of what you experience as perplexity arises
because new forces first have to gather and form
in you.** You experience this as being so difficult only
because you are constantly commenting or because
you let go of being present for your state of being
much too early and seek distraction.

Remain playful and present, even when it is difficult. Cheerfulness is an opening, through which many new things can flow in.

Wind your way, and feel your way through the world. See, smell, and taste the way animals do, in natural presence.
Then return to your daily work as to your home port, where you want to seduce and nurture a power that you have seen or experienced.

May every act be a thought. If you fully succeed in achieving this presence for even just five minutes, the day gets its true shining.
May this day be like your dawn, in which you begin to see and understand yet another piece of yourself and of the world.

Do it fully and learn to let go, so that things can occur in you all by themselves.
You say that all this is too difficult and almost impossible? Direct your defiance against the old patterns in you and not against the new. Use your defiance as a strong power against the old distractions.

It is only so difficult to let go because you have learned differently for so long. Nobody has said that it is easy. **But once you have it, then it is easy. Your life then finds its fulfillment.**

Practice this consciousness, as if you wanted to climb a mountain that has never been climbed by anyone before.

In this way, the Divine can be anchored within you and recognition takes place.

Ya azim.

Cheerfulness is an opening,
through which many new things can flow in.

Abstract Art

Successful abstraction is a higher art than successful illustration. There are hardly any examples of this, but the spirit of the times longs for it. Abstraction requires a special power of awareness and precision.

Reach out with all your senses and wait until something is activated inside. Then follow the laws of color and the lines that emerge.
The art of the new age arises from this abstraction. It could also be called a condensation or a concretion. Many artists have struggled with this, but its true birth has not yet occurred.

New icons will be born, as will a new power of seeing and forming, giving direction to the Zeitgeist. **Art is to a great degree involved in the field creation for a new era.**

When true abstraction is fully implemented, a new process of inner seeing opens up. Combined with this new power of seeing, things in reality also connect in a new way. Your body and mind opened up to a new frequency of reality. You are then, to a very high degree, both the new Creation and the Creator. You understand how Creation and what is created have the same origin.

This effort and this work require great perseverance on your part, as well as a spirit of playfulness, with which you encompass the birth process itself. It is not only expressed on your canvas and in your work, but little by little it leads to a new birth and a new state of existence within you.

Ya azim.

Combined with a new power of seeing,
things in reality connect in a new way.

Wishes are Signposts to God

Peace only occurs when your wishes, longings and desires have become still. It is only when all wishes fall silent that full peace can be seen and understood.

The yogi comes to the conclusion of renouncing the world. For him, all wishes and desires are only the deceit and illusion of an unconscious soul, which has not seen the Divine.
But that, too, is escapism.

The world was created in its abundance for peace to shine in this abundance. Become aware of your true wishes and connect with their possible realization. Call out to the universal certainty of success.

As long as you see your wishes as something exterior and want to fulfill them from the outside, you will not be able to find the peace of your soul.

You will understand peace when you have come into contact with universal love. It lies within your self and it cannot be found anywhere else.

Although love is one of the most frequently used words, only very few know what love is.

Most people believe that love is something that one must receive, instead of seeing that it is a principle of Creation that wants to be seen and realized.

Learn to recognize the laws that let you become a focal point for all lovers, instead of screaming for love like a blackmailer.

Divine consciousness has not created your needs in order for you to renounce them. At the same time, it does not create any needs in order for you to succumb to them, but so that you see them as signposts for your life and learn from them.

Know that every need, every wish, and every longing was created by you, yourself. It is your teacher and is in the service of a higher insight.

Once you see this, you are able to let go. You enter into a new status of apprenticeship.
Every inner desire is a signpost to God. The realization of peace is based on trust in the fulfillment

167

that already exists within the desire. You would not have this desire in you, if this fulfillment did not exist.

That is a very joyous message.

Blessed be your wishes and desires. Ya azim.

Every inner desire is a signpost to God.

Mind and Eros

Eros is a universal process. It has its own laws that must be learned.

Train yourself in your presence for each other and for the world.
The world is full of answers for each of you. In order to hear them, you only need to know and ask the questions that you truly have.

A large part of the problem consists of the habit of suppressing the erotic reality from your lives. The problems come from the sluggishness of the mind, when it does not want to open up to the world. If you have a problem, it is almost always the result of closing off the erotic and encompassing reality of the world.

Know that there is an answer for every problem. Problems in relationships are, as rule, a bastion against Eros and against truth.

As long as you identify with your problems, you are like a piece of wood, drifting in front of the wall of a dam, which has lost its connection to the cosmic energy and therefore constantly goes around in circles. Give it the kick that it needs from the world, and a new path will open up for it.

If you have a problem, do not identify with it. Instead, allow the world to come in. See your problem as your own very special guideline for your personal development and unfolding. If you do not hold on to your problem, then the answering power of life can enter you and lead you in a new direction.

As a seedling penetrates through a layer of asphalt, it also experiences friction and resistance, and it also casts off its skin.
But it is not aware of the trap of constantly commenting on and judging oneself, which makes a problem so sluggish and heavy in the first place.
Rid yourselves of this sluggish mass.

Since you are in a body, the answering power is always connected to the powers of Eros.

Eros itself is the flow of bodily life. Stop resisting your own erotic reality.

Eros cannot exist permanently without the Mind. And a living Mind cannot exist permanently without Eros.

Eros and religion have the same goal and the same source. Become aware of the sacred quality of life, and the emerging joy in your cells can begin to dance in you. The insight that life wants you to have can only come to you through an open body.

The entire biosphere begins to rejoice when undisguised encounters between men and women can occur without conditions, without fixated relationships, without demands or neediness. They arise from existence itself. May today be in the service of this existence.

I am with you. Ya azim.

Eros cannot exist permanently without the Mind. And a living Mind cannot exist permanently without Eros.

The Collective Messiah

A new collective Messiah is waiting to be recognized and realized. It is a gestalt that carries redemption and salvation. It arises from the deepening willingness of the individual to take a stand against fear. This is not an act of courage, but one of an ever-deepening ability to see and understand.

Fear results in isolation and violence.
The decision to take a stand against fear and for trust awakens a high level of knowledge in you, which to a great extent can protect you against violence.

Today, there will be no more individual figures of redemption. It no longer corresponds to the spirit of the times. Yet there is a spiritual field which can be accessed and that carries the powers of salvation within it.

Connect with the feeling that the world and the atmosphere are filled with the information for the new field. Here lies the breath and the heartbeat of the Goddess, who is pushing toward a new fulfillment. Open your cells consciously to this new frequency.

Let your devotion and your prayer become a cellular process that is accompanied by consciousness and that fills your entire body.

Follow the processes that open your body consciously. Fearful thoughts have long closed off the body; here you can study the entire history of your culture.

If you follow the opening and rediscover your true sensual energies, you will gain knowledge from prehistoric times. You will feel the dawn of a new culture in your body.

You are still frightened by the immensity of the forces.

Violence is the result of thousands of years of suppressing the natural forces in you and in the world.

Once you have found the power to integrate the immensity of the forces within you, you have found the gentle power of the formation of a new culture.

Throw overboard your false sense of reason, which always stops you from letting your body speak. Have the courage to stand up for your own truth, your beauty, and the depth of your being. Leave behind what makes you fearful and conformist.

Follow everything with the understanding eye of your mind. You will then rediscover the foundation of a more encompassing state of being. This is a great discovery. This is how the field of a collective Messiah is born; this is how the Goddess can be born anew on earth.

Ya azim.

Taking a stand against fear and for trust awakens a high level of knowledge in you, which to a great extent can protect you against violence.

The Birth of Truth

The greatest task that needs to be accomplished today is the return to the foundation of truth.

It is as if you were digging for groundwater in a desert in which there has been no water for a long time. It takes a certain effort to get rid of the debris, for you have used a lot of your own energy to pile it up. A lot of your own power is now bound in this debris.

Sometimes the search for one's innermost truth elicits fear, for ever since the emergence of patriarchy, truth seekers have always been punished. Instead, since thousands of years, people prefer to remain entrapped and to use their swords, their malice and their revenge against anything that looks like truth.

This is the reason for the strong trembling, the fear and the resistance that arise as soon as you approach your own truth. It also makes you begin to destroy in others what you actually want to love. To calm your fears, you follow false images of love and community.

What seems so threatening, so powerful and consuming to you is the aspect of the Goddess that was suppressed for thousands of years. Now storms, earthquakes and wars sweep over one country after the other. It is the long suppressed aspect of the Goddess, the long suppressed and molested truth, that makes its presence felt. She demands of you a dedication and participation in the world, which you have avoided for a long time.

Wars arise from suppressed truth; never from truth itself.

Before you arrive at the core of your truth, you have to look into the painful history of much suppressed rage, fear, revenge, hatred, envy and pretense.
Nobody likes to do this, and therefore you protect yourselves from each other and from yourselves through an ideological veneer of normality and reason.

But go through that. Stop pointing your sword only at others, but point it at your own fearful ghosts, like someone who fights dragons. Rediscover your own natural landscape.

Know that an incredibly beautiful face of truth and of the world is waiting for you, a face that you will love infinitely. Your heart will fill with love of yourself and love of the world, in a way that you have long since forgotten.

Here lies your greatest protection. Fear disappears when you reach the core of truth. At the core of truth, infinite protection for the life forces lies waiting for you.

An eternal veil of fear will lift from you and your eye will become seeing.

When you touch this foundation, the conscious choice is made to live in a sacred way. You then guide your steps and your will in this world with courage. Your voice will rise up with a new force and a deeply known and deeply forgotten song will resonate over the earth.

Ideologies can be fought and killed. But truth itself has an infinite power and will to survive. It wants to clear the way and awaken fully in you, so that no enemy can penetrate and destroy it.

That is the historic awakening of original Creation in you, with a new zeitgeist and a new power. Enter into this birth process fully. There is no more time to lose. Help to create communities, in which this birth process can occur.

Fear disappears
when you reach the core of truth.

What To Do in These Difficult Times

I greet this day. I greet the spirit of universal love.

I greet the community of all those who love.

You ask what you can do in these difficult times?

Be the self that you are meant to be, in the large, encompassing, universal sense. This means that you naturally let go of arrogance, inferiority, vanity and false morals. Your connection with your higher self is also your best protection against jealousy, comparison, fear of abandonment, and false competition.

True peace work is the greatest and most important profession that you can pursue today. The truth of your heart is your most reliable signpost. Study the laws through which community arises. The world cries out for survival knowledge that comes from trust.

During these times, there is no hunger that is as great as the hunger for true community. Do not wait until it is there for you, but contribute with all your power to making it happen, wherever you are.

Your own source is your protection. It is activated immediately when you find your natural place in the universe and rediscover your task.
The world wants to assemble in you and be recognized by you.

Once you have rediscovered your own universal task, the entire universe is the placenta for your work. The greater the task is that you take on, the more power will flow toward you if your action and will is the will of the universe.

The only thing that you must do is to be awake and listen to the voice of your heart. Protect it from old habits and from false morals. Examine your dark side with courage; it wants to be recognized and transformed.

If you can solve your problem, you are solving it as a representative for many. Take farewell of feelings of guilt and bad conscience, for they only evoke anger at the truth within you.

Nurture the power of trust by holding conscious thoughts. They are the nourishment that the new world needs so that its germinating power can grow in you.

I wish you all the best.

*Be the self that you are meant to be,
in the large, encompassing, universal sense.*

The Assignment

It never rains but it pours. The opposite is also true.

The more you learn not to identify with your fortune or your misfortune, the easier you can enter the gate that leads you to higher knowledge of life. Here, you find something that connects you with the wisdom of your own heart.

Happiness and misery pave the way to your true assignment.

Find your life assignment. Hear your assignment again. Live your assignment. Be your assignment.

Within your assignment lies your highest happiness, your purpose, your power, your security, your path and your promise.

Be who you are, and do not judge yourself for your weaknesses.
Often, your very special purpose, your very special strength, beauty and truth lie hidden behind your seeming weakness. Be who you are.

That is your greatest and most courageous contribution to the creation of peace. It connects you with the source of eternal life.

God and you have both chosen it. Even if you often find it difficult to believe. Your higher self has chosen and created your higher reality and so has God.

Your higher inner voice knows why you are here. The Divine wants to work through you. And yet it is you who are taking, choosing and realizing this path. For you are an aspect of the Divine, of the whole.

Only the ego has a strange idea of self-realization and of doing its own work, of subjectivity and objectivity.

There is no subject that is cut off from the whole. But there is also no subject that is operating behind all things. It is only through the connection with the whole that the whole can realize itself.

Walk in this connection and you are walking the path of your perfection. If you choose the path of the ego, you choose the path of abandonment and destruction. For only what is separated can die.

If you walk the path of the higher self and of connection, you walk the path of eternal life.

Walk your path of becoming and do not identify with the powers of the ego. Then much more joy of life and abundance can come to you, and you are protected by your cosmic home and eternity.

Ya azim.

Be who your are.
This connects you to the source of eternal life.

Do Not Identify

The parable of the stove.

What to do in a difficult situation?
Do not identify.

Life always has an answer ready for you.

But the answer can only reach you if you have learned to remain in a non-identified state, even in difficult situations.

That is the greatest art that needs to be learned.
There is a deeper meaning behind everything that you experience. Your illness is also an attempt to achieve a reconnection with the whole. It is an indication that your mental and spiritual awareness now needs to focus on areas that you normally do not focus on.

The lack of connection almost always comes from false attachment. You are attached to thoughts, ideas or situations that cannot guide your mind and your spirit toward freedom.

The first step is: become a witness!

The worst thing is if the lack of connection is not noticed. The ego is willing to undertake much in order to cover up the real connections.

So at this moment you are disconnected. Become aware of this, inform the universe, and be ready to wait for an answer.

In a disconnected state, of course the most difficult thing is to trust that an answer will come. Direct your attention on how you can return to a space of trust. The easiest way for this to occur is if you succeed in truly becoming still for a moment. **The greater connection can occur easiest within the space of true stillness.** Many Yoga masters knew this.

When you want to enter into the space of stillness, you will notice where you are attached.

Let ME speak in a parable.
You want to move the gas stove closer to you so that you can warm yourself better. The stove will not budge. You push and shove and waste a lot of energy. You get annoyed and angry. And you think:

it's the stove's fault. Or else you fall into self-pity because you're a loser. When you have ranted and raved long enough in your hopeless desperation, you suddenly stop.

Now the answer can come to you. You notice that the stove has gotten stuck in the carpet, and you now focus your attention on how to get it unstuck. If you need help, you will get help. Suddenly, everything is easy.

Things are very similar in the cosmic space. In a state of disconnection you rage inside an invisible cage, but one that has a clear pattern. Help does not come until the moment when stillness lets you enter into the space of perception. It is a certain thought, an idea, that has gotten stuck. When you have become aware of it, you can either solve it yourself, or ask for help if you need it.

It is often the body itself that needs help. Often, you can only enter a state of higher frequency and awareness if you have given it certain substances or drugs. Without that, you do not succeed in concentrating. But if this is practiced consistently, it

187

leads to attachment, fixation and dependency, not to freedom. It creates fear in you, where it does not belong.

When you feel this, give full attention to your body.

Take care to stay so physically healthy that your mind is as free and independent as possible, so that it becomes open to the cosmic voice of life.

When I say this, then I am not speaking of asceticism or renunciation. The physical abundance of life is there to be used. But it should be used so that it does not lead to dependency.

Do not believe in these attachments. Shake them off as you would shake off fetters that are too constricting. This is true for old habits of behavior as well as for love.

At first it requires yearlong training, **but then it naturally leads to a constant connection.**
When you wake up in the morning, this connection gives you the thoughts that gladly accompany you during this day.

In this way you find the thoughts for which you want to live, for which you like to love and work, because they lead you to permanent connection and love.

Ya azim.

Help does not come until
the moment when stillness
lets you enter into the space of perception.

Inner Preparation

Focus on essentials. Practice patience that comes from seeing. Connect with the awareness that your third eye is a seeing organ.

On the one hand, you need to prepare yourself intellectually for taking a leap, so that you know what it is all about, recognize yourself, and focus on what is essential.
On the other hand, there is the energetic preparation. Learn to allow your cells and your body to enter into a state of openness, a state of awareness, and at the same time a state of elasticity, so that you are ready to take a leap at all times.

A person who is free of fear is ready to take a leap at any second.

Gather this elasticity within yourself. Act only when you know that the time to act has come.

Know that all your cells are held together through consciousness and that they constantly follow certain information and energy lines.

It is as if they follow a post-hypnotic order that you yourself have once given to them and that you can rediscover and change. The only pathway to change that always works is the path of self-knowledge. Do not comment on yourself, but see.

What is it that is stopping you from saying and following the truth? The more you truly want to know, the more enduring your decision is, and the gentler you are embedded in your own trusting, the further your new power and development can take you.

Trust is also a decision that you make here and now. In the surroundings that you have created, what reasons are there to distrust?

If you do not yet trust, then become aware of why this is so. Do not focus on your personal knots and problems too soon. First, create this energetic and conscious space, and you will notice how much intelligence, joy of life, curiosity, health and power begins to flow, simply because of this decision.

From this aspect, you can now perceive the healing

that needs to occur for you personally, karmically or historically.

Without this background, focusing on your faults and weaknesses only generates fear.

Once you notice the fear and feel how it transforms into interest and a desire to know, then you are on the right path.

First, find the courage to trust again and to know. Become aware of how much, over the millennia, the human being as a species has blocked his access to this simple path.

Do not judge yourself and your fellow human beings for this, but prepare to take the steps toward change. Always see your healing from this overall historic perspective, for then the cosmic force and source that you need can flow toward you.

Thank you and ya azim.

Once you notice the fear and feel how it transforms into interest and a desire to know, then you are on the right path.

Your Step toward World Peace

There is a cruel war raging in Chechnya as well as in many other countries on earth. I ask the divine light of life to come to me and speak in all your aspects of encompassing love. I ask for the power and the intelligence that teaches us how we can understand and actualize the aspects of a possible global peace in ourselves. May this give birth to the power to act that can bring peace to this planet. I ask for the information that now is of importance to all of us and that we can use.

There is only **one** existence.
As long as you believe in your own distress, you reinforce the global field of distress.

Use the freedom that you have and let go of believing in your suffering. Do this on behalf of all those who now do not have this freedom and this power and who urgently need your help.
Use your rage to discard the old.
Allow the laws of field creation to take effect in you and throw out all fear. It is only through this decision that you will be able to heal your past.

It is also only through this decision, through which I can work through you, that you will be able to solve your own personal issues around love, alcohol or cigarettes.

There is healing only if you accept love.
Connect with the power of calm and perception that leads to true seeing.

Notice that trust is an active step that you can and must decide to take, here and now. Notice that trust can be learned.

Notice that it is necessary for you to take the step of trust in order for the divine source of healing and insight to be able to come to you.

Do not follow fear. Do not follow anger.
Follow the light of trust within you.
Trust is the action that you must take; the rest can then occur by itself at the given time.

Notice that distrust consists of your own conscious or unconscious negative thoughts that you do not want anyone to discover.

But there is a level of light within trust, where these thoughts are transformed and disappear all by themselves, because there is something higher, more encompassing and more exciting.

It is only when you are connected to the power of trust that you will be able to have the success that you desire. Seek out, here and now, with all your power, those thoughts that give you back your basic trust.

These are thoughts of a vital and committed love, thoughts of truth, thoughts of your inner beauty.
You will notice that only they have the power of survival and lead to the knowledge that you need for your healing.

Take leave of fear. Enter into the state of encompassing love. Currently, that is the highest and most encompassing step toward world peace that you can take.

It is so simple, so elementary and so true. Become aware of your inner light, which comes from trust, and follow it. The rest occurs all by itself.

As soon as you realize that the freedom of a life that is fully lived is within you, here and now, and that you can choose trust, peace and happiness, you strengthen a global field of trust, which also can take effect in areas of crisis.

Become a bringer of light by studying these laws.

Ya azim.

It is so simple, elementary and true.
Become aware of your inner light,
which comes from trust, and follow it.
The rest occurs all by itself.

Dealing with Your Inner Enemy

It is time to take a powerful step forward.

Do not give your faults and weaknesses any more nourishment. When you begin to see them and also to look into the dark cellars where you have never looked, then they have the habit of first of all inflating themselves out of all proportion.

When fear, jealousy or hatred begin to beleaguer you, do not allow this. Choose what you devote yourself to.

It makes no sense to blindly give in to your inner enemies and then, on top of it all, to believe that your surroundings are to blame for this.

Use your willingness to fight, which you used to apply externally, against your inner enemies. And above all, do not believe that you are a victim. You are not a victim, but a perpetrator of your life.

Inside, your fight needs new strategies. It is no longer enough to fight against something. If you have managed to silence one enemy, then somewhere else another one gets up. This is true both on the inside and the outside. The old strategies of extermination no longer work, just as bloodshed can never truly be a solution.

Recognize the extent to which cruelty is born of desperation. Transform your own wild energy, which wants to explode in blind rage, into power and presence.

Step into perception.
Take back your energies.

Dare to look your enemy in the face. Discover his true face behind the many masks. Recognize that your enemy is a part of your self: an abandoned, neglected and unredeemed part of your life.

Now you will recognize the true meaning and power of reconciliation. At the deepest level, healing truly occurs through reconciliation.

This reconciliation can only occur by creating a path of transformation for your enemy so that he can find his original power again.

Step into vision. Go to where your enemy leaves all by himself, or where he gets a right to live within you that serves the whole.

In many of your enemies you will find the distorted and disfigured face of your age-old friends.

When you discover within what needs to be done, then your external power and effectiveness will skyrocket. There is healing knowledge within you that is urgently needed. Call upon it.

Ya azim.

Use your willingness to fight, which you used to apply externally, against your inner enemies. And above all, do not believe that you are a victim.
You are not a victim, but a perpetrator of your life.

Karmic Healing

There are dark places in your lives. There are basements in your soul that you would prefer not to look into. They should be cleared out and cleaned.

Whenever you enter into the truly dark zones of your overall karmic self, the question will arise in you:
Why should I go there?
Why should I look at that?
Is it not enough, if I now make a decision for good in this life?

This path is not enough for encompassing and global healing work. Nor is it enough for your true inner healing and liberation.

Try to find the point where you became a perpetrator. Or try to find the point when and where you became a victim.

At first, when you go back into your karmic history, different incarnations will surface and you will see that, in a certain way, one and the same topic runs through them all.

At some point you come back to the place of origin. You will see when and why you stepped into the karmic dance of victim and perpetrator for the first time.

This point is like a very personal needle's eye.
At this cosmic point, you will find the reasons for the split into being a victim and a perpetrator, and you will realize what it means to you personally to make a decision to lead a good and sacred life.
Beyond this point, the full cosmic healing knowledge opens up to you. When you have passed through this point, memory returns as does the cosmic shining that makes you knowing.

The planet now again begins to shine, you recognize your home again, which otherwise only opened up after the moment of your death.

Find the ring of knowledge again, find the motivation that guided you originally, and become aware of what made you abandon this knowledge. You thereby dissolve not only your personal hypnosis, but you begin to open an iron ring of hypnosis that has encircled the entire planet. It is the ring of hypnosis and fear, of forgetting and violence, which has led to mutilation, torture, murder, misery and suffering.

The most important point is this: do not identify yourself with anything. Misery began when people began to identify themselves with something that they are not.

You will see that it is easier for perpetrator souls not to become identified. They could only carry out their deed by keeping their hearts closed. When your heart now begins to open, a new sadness and a new pain will arise. You feel vulnerable, unsure of yourself, almost child-like. Here, too, it is important not to identify yourself.

Practice the art of non-identification with an open heart. Enter into the great compassion that this planet needs. But do not let yourself be driven to hopelessness.

Allow this; it is like an inner cleansing that frees your body and your spirit from old waste. Your heart now wants to open up, it wants to become seeing. It wants to remove the ring of guilt from itself that for so long has given you the feeling that you may not really open your heart. But now you are here for reasons of love. And you know what that is from the cosmic spaces where you came from.

Realize it here and do not wait any longer for your next life. Recognize why you are here.

The most important point is this:
do not identify yourself with anything.

I Am an Organ of God

I am an organ of God.

I strengthen this image as often as I can. I increasingly let it become a part of my true nature.

I inform my unconscious through this image. I connect with the vision of a sacred life that I can actually live. May my life be my prayer.

Vision carries great power. There is nothing more powerful than a vision with which I am fully connected.

The more my vision becomes second nature to me, the more reality it can attract.
The more committed I am to my vision, the more it supports me, also in difficult situations.
The more encompassing my vision becomes, the more it becomes a part of the creative healing process in the world.

In this way I take leave of all the old images of a religion that was connected to a punishing God.

I am an organ of God. As this organ, I seek and find God inside myself. I here find the mirror of a perfect world. Here lies the connection between my own deepest will and the will of divine power.

To recognize, see and realize God inside oneself is a decision that one makes. Great trust is born of this decision.

It is with an unstoppable longing that this divine power in me wants to realize a world of peace, community, spiritual presence and sensual joy. I walk this path with this power. I let myself be guided by it. It is what helps me to leave fear behind and to walk the path of trust.

I recognize that God is with me by a great inner joy and sense of security, which paves the way for me through all difficulties.

This divine power connects me with all existence. It is a revolutionary power, which keeps me connected with truth, since I no longer need to fear any truth.

Being an organ of God connects me with the community of all living beings, wherever I am. That is the source of the transformation that will initiate historic change.

Thank you and Amen.

The divine power connects me with all existence.
It is a revolutionary power,
which keeps me connected with truth,
since I no longer need to fear any truth.

Truth and Healing

When people come together in truth, healing occurs. You create trust when you establish truth.

Know that you always have cosmic support if you stay with the truth. The divine source in you - that is the truth in you. As long as we allow ourselves to lie now and then, we contribute to war, fear and violence.

When people come together in truth, healing occurs. Do not give way to dissimulation, but follow the truth and your life will change.

Do not wait any longer for it to change. It changes all on its own when you decide to stay with the truth.

So you are challenged to swim against the current. You ask where you can get the power to do that.

The power is there all by itself, once you have made an inner decision for truth.
Fear and lies are twins. Truth has the power to overcome fear.

If you have made an inner decision for truth, you will find the power and the knowledge needed to say things so that they have an effect.

It is not a question of throwing the truth at every person. It is an inner decision that makes me take a look at those areas within me that I have so far refused to have anything to do with.
It is an inner decision to want to know the truth. I now begin to see and recognize who I am – also in areas that I previously did not want to know about.

The path of participation in the fate of others begins with a connection to truth.

I step into the center of my own actions and I take full responsibility.

I choose the path of trust and truth and thus enter into sacred life.

I trust the inner guidance that comes from these sources.

Ya azim. Blessed be the love of truth.

Follow truth
and your life will change.
Do not wait any longer for it to change.
It changes all on its own,
when you choose the truth.

The Garden of Eden

Imagine that you are standing at a gateway of time. This gateway is the opening to Paradise. You go through it, and you look into another world.
It is truly the Garden of Eden.

It already exists as a latent reality. Live in the awareness of this higher presence. Hear the call of the birds, plants, animals, and angels. They are waiting for the human being.

A whole world, within you and around you, wants to reveal itself to you.
Recognize your own higher image within yourself. It exists already now, at this moment. Becoming aware of it is a matter of frequency and opening.

The Garden of Eden can only be realized if you follow the path of trust. It occurs and manifests out of the world of connection.

The Garden of Eden is based on the principles of complementarity, insight, revealing oneself, and trust.

The human being must decide to step out of the world of separation.

Make sure that the information you send out is unambiguous. Make sure that you do not wish for something different than what you say in public. Send your information into the world and wait for the world to answer.

To succeed also means to follow, and success is the result of information that we send into the world.

Be like a dolphin. Dolphins cannot lie.

Animals, plants, rocks, elements and spiritual beings are waiting for human beings to be connected to the whole and to live fully in truth.

We can then together walk down the common path of trust and then the feast of revelation can begin.

Open the gate, also in the area of love between humans. This is the determining gate: lies or truth, fear or trust, constriction or freedom, reaction or perception, accusations or healing?

Do not wait for others. Begin with your own truth. The Divine in you will take care of the rest.

But seek ye first the kingdom of God, and his righteousness; and all these things shall be added unto you.

Ya azim.

Do not wait for others.
Begin with your own truth.
The Divine in you will take care of the rest.

Seeing with the Heart

When you begin to see with your heart, then the heart of the earth can also heal. And when the heart of the earth begins to heal, then the heart of the entire female gender can heal and take on the function and the true love that is its very own.

When you have become seeing with your heart, you will become an ecologist, a healer, a revolutionary, and a true lover.

Then the true healing of the male gender can begin. New healing roles can then be seen and received.

Now that you are increasingly finding the calm of perception and the seeing that comes from the third eye, you can also begin to see with your heart. You can let your heart speak.

Your seeing heart finds the power, the courage and perseverance to look deep into your own core.

You will notice how much longing, wishes and desires that you thought were your own, fall away.

Everything that you have thought and felt suddenly becomes infinitely small.

The seeing heart opens up a new space. The sobriety and the true magnitude of universal love can enter in.

You will notice all the things that you have done to avoid seeing the pain of the earth. With a seeing heart you will see the pain and the sorrow of the earth, but it will not make you resigned; instead, answers will come to you. You realize what you need to do and you no longer doubt that you will do it.

With a seeing heart you know that your full healing will have a global effect, and that you are becoming a being that is thinking and acting globally.
With a seeing heart there is no longer any competition, jealousy or hatred, for you are connected with the knowledge that comes from universal love.
With a seeing heart there is still grief, compassion, sympathy, pain and sacred rage. But above all these, there is the connection and the happiness that comes from love and from the possibilities inherent in this existence.

God is love. You will find this source also in pain and in distress. It has a healing power, wherever you are.

These sources of perception will provide you with an ever-greater power to act, in order to increase the ability to experience joy and love. For it is only this power to act that can heal this planet.

In the name of your power and your ability to love; in the name of your open heart.

Ya azim.

> *The seeing heart finds the power,*
> *the courage and the perseverance*
> *to look deep into your own core.*

VERLAG MEIGA
For a Future Without War

Sabine Lichtenfels
GRACE
Pilgrimage for a Future without War
ISBN: 978-3-927266-25-4, 262 pages

Dieter Duhm
The Sacred Matrix
From the Matrix of Violence to the Matrix of Life
ISBN: 978-3-927266-16-2, 370 pages

Dieter Duhm
Future without War
Theory of Global Healing
ISBN: 978-3-927266-24-7, 120 pages

More about Sabine Lichtenfels:
www.sabine-lichtenfels.com